Natural
Wonders
— *of* —

Connecticut
&
Rhode Island

Natural
Wonders
—— of ——
Connecticut
&
Rhode Island

A Guide to
Parks, Preserves
& Wild Places

Carol F. Henshaw

Illustrated by Lois Leonard Stock

Country Roads Press

CASTINE • MAINE

Natural Wonders of Connecticut & Rhode Island:
A Guide to Parks, Preserves & Wild Places
© 1995 by Carol Fairfield Henshaw. All rights reserved.

Grateful acknowledgment is made to Random House, Inc., for permission to quote passages from *Reflections from the North Country* by Sigurd F. Olson. Published by Alfred A. Knopf, Inc., New York, and by Random House of Canada Limited in Toronto.

Grateful acknowledgment is also made to the University of Connecticut Libraries for permission to quote passages from *A Naturalist Buys an Old Farm* by Edwin Way Teale, copyright 1974 by Edwin Way Teale, published by Dodd, Mead & Company, New York.

Published by Country Roads Press
P.O. Box 286, Lower Main Street
Castine, Maine 04421

Text and cover design by Studio 3, Ellsworth, Maine.
Cover photograph courtesy of Rhode Island Tourism Division.
Illustrations by Lois Leonard Stock.
Typesetting by Typeworks, Belfast, Maine.

ISBN 1-56626-079-5

Library of Congress Cataloging-in-Publication Data

Henshaw, Carol Fairfield.
    Natural wonders of Connecticut and Rhode Island : a guide to parks, preserves, and wild places / Carol Fairfield Henshaw ; illustrator, Lois Leonard Stock.
        p.   cm.
    Includes bibliographical references and index.
    ISBN 1-56626-079-5 : $9.95
        1. Connecticut – Guidebooks.   2. Natural history – Connecticut – Guidebooks.   3. Natural areas – Connecticut – Guidebooks.
    4. Parks – Connecticut – Guidebooks.   5. Botanical gardens – Connecticut – Guidebooks.   6. Rhode Island – Guidebooks.
    7. Natural history – Guidebooks.   8. Natural areas – Rhode Island – Guidebooks.   9. Parks – Rhode Island – Guidebooks.
    10. Botanical gardens – Rhode Island – Guidebooks.   I. Title.
    F92.3.H46 1995
    917.4604′43 – dc20   94-37491
                                                                              CIP

Printed in the United States of America.
10 9 8 7 6 5 4 3 2 1

To
the memory of my parents,
Maxine Fairfield and Herbert Edward Henshaw,
who first introduced me
to the beauty and wonders of the natural world,
and
to all those who love the land and its wildlife.

Contents

7 THE COAST

Acknowledgments

I wish to thank all those persons who during the past year have helped in the gathering of information and the writing of this book.

First, I want to thank Milly Bohannah, Instructor of English at the University of New Haven, and my good friend since college days, who not only did the word processing, but also edited the text and provided moral support when needed.

I also wish to thank John Florian, Editorial Director of *Northeast Outdoors*, the publication that first gave me an opportunity to write about camping, travel, and nature-related subjects in the Northeast. Some of the material included in the entries on Kent Falls, Lake Waramaug, Squantz Pond, and Devil's Hopyard State Parks in Connecticut and Beavertail State Park and Conanicut Island in Rhode Island originally appeared in the pages of *Northeast Outdoors*, which is published in Waterbury, Connecticut.

I am also indebted to the personnel of the Connecticut State Parks Division of the Department of Environmental Protection, the Division of Parks and Recreation of the Rhode Island Department of Environmental Management, the Sharon Audubon Center, Flanders Nature Center, and the Audubon Society of Rhode Island for answering questions and furnishing informative material.

Special thanks go to Jeff Greenwood, Museum Director at the White Memorial Foundation and Conservation Center, who answered questions and provided me with information on the species of birds, wildflowers, and mammals one might see on White Memorial Foundation lands.

I also wish to express my appreciation to Sherman Kent, President of the Connecticut Audubon Society, and Gail Even, Office Manager at the Hartford Center of the Connecticut Audubon Society, for their assistance with this guide.

In addition, I wish to thank Donna Lindgren, Executive Director of the Ansonia Nature Center, and Chuck Collinge, an outdoor writer and part-time ranger at the center, for the information they provided about the center and the birds and other wildlife to be seen there.

Finally, I am grateful to Richard Fyffe, Humanities Bibliographer and Curator of Literary Archives at the Homer Babbidge Library, for his assistance with the entry on Trail Wood, the Edwin Way Teale Memorial Sanctuary.

You all helped to make this book possible.

Introduction

Without love of the land,
conservation lacks meaning and purpose,
for only in a deep and inherent feeling for the land
can there be dedication in preserving it.

—Sigurd F. Olson
Reflections from the North Country

This is a book about special places in Connecticut and Rhode Island—parks, nature centers, and wildlife refuges—that exist today, safe from the ravages of commercial development, because of those who so loved the land that they worked and fought political battles to ensure its preservation.

In Connecticut and Rhode Island, state and private organizations continue the struggle to preserve our natural environment and to restore coastal and inland bodies of water and streams that have been polluted by those who were more motivated by greed than by a love of the land.

Extraordinary individuals have devoted their lives to ensuring the preservation of land for future generations of men and wildlife. Connecticut is deeply indebted to two residents of Litchfield, Alan C. White and his sister May, who in 1908 set out to preserve the beauty of Bantam Lake and the surrounding countryside for the public to enjoy. Today the White Memorial Foundation and Conservation Center in Litchfield manages some 4,000 acres. Two outstanding state parks, Kent Falls and Macedonia Brook, were also gifts of the foundation set up by the Whites.

Probably the most difficult task in writing this guide was selecting the parks and wildlife refuges to be included. I have chosen my favorite destinations, but there are many special places in both states, and some, regrettably, had to be left out. Additional natural areas of special interest may be found in the preserves of The Nature Conservancy. For a guide to these areas in Connecticut, refer to *Country Walks in Connecticut: A Guide to The Nature Conservancy Preserves* by Susan D. Cooley.

The entries are, in general, arranged geographically from north to south and from west to east. They are a guide to some of the best places for nature walks, bird-watching, hiking, canoeing, cross-country skiing, and nature photography. You'll also find special places to swim, camp, or enjoy a picnic.

Whether you visit a state park or a private nature center, it is important to remember that loving the land means leaving no litter behind and not disturbing any plants or animals you find there. A policy of "carry out what you carry in" has been instituted in all Connecticut state parks, which now have recycling stations where you deposit glass, cans, plastic items, and trash in separate bins.

SOME WORDS OF CAUTION

Hiking in both Connecticut and Rhode Island requires a few precautions. Because of the incidence of rabies in wild animals, you are advised not to approach raccoons, skunks, or foxes, especially if the animal appears to be sick or is behaving in a strange manner.

In addition, it is wise to protect yourself against being bitten by deer ticks, which can carry Lyme disease. Ticks are most prevalent in May, June, and July. When hiking in wooded or brushy areas, wearing light colors helps you spot any ticks that attach themselves to your clothing. Hikers are also advised to wear hats, long pants, and shirts, and to tuck pant legs into socks or boots and shirts into pants. On a very hot summer day, you may prefer just to check your skin for ticks after the hike or to use insect repellent containing DEET.

All the places included in this guide are relatively safe areas to be in. However, when visiting parks that are easily accessible from large urban areas, you should use the same caution that you would use in a city and avoid hiking alone in isolated areas.

Because water conditions in rivers and streams can change rapidly, it is always wise to scout a stream or to check with local authorities before embarking on a canoe trip.

CONNECTICUT

1

The Litchfield Hills

No matter how tightly the body may be chained
to the wheel of daily duties,
the spirit is free if it so pleases,
to cancel space and to bear itself away
from noise and vexation
into the secret places of the mountains.

—Frank Bolles
At the North of Bearcamp Water

To the area that is now the town of Kent in northwestern Connecticut, the Indians gave the name The Place Beyond the Mountains. The Litchfield Hills are the foothills of the Berkshires. While their altitude would not impress anyone familiar with mountains (Mount Frissell at 2,380 feet is the highest point in Connecticut), these rugged hills have a special beauty that draws you back again and again to this part of the state.

Within the boundaries of Kent, 4,000 acres have been preserved as state parks and public lands, including Lake

Waramaug State Park, Macedonia Brook State Park, and Kent Falls State Park.

This is the region where you will find hills to climb, deep ravines, waterfalls, sparkling streams, alpine lakes, and deep, cool forests of hemlock, beech, maple, and hickory. Here the Appalachian Trail passes through the state, and the Housatonic River flows between the hills, passing under a historic covered bridge (Bulls Bridge) in Kent.

In Litchfield, you can explore the trails of the state's largest wildlife refuge at the White Memorial Foundation and Conservation Center.

This part of Connecticut is special at any time of year. In winter it often has snow when the ground is bare in other parts of the state. You can get out and see wildlife, or at least find their tracks, by taking to the trails on cross-country skis or snowshoes. In spring, when the hills are clad in delicate shades of green, you may come to see the cascading waterfall in Kent Falls State Park, observe wildflowers in bloom, or bird-watch at a time when great flocks are migrating north through the valleys.

Summer is a time for swimming and picnics, but it is perhaps in fall that the Litchfield Hills are most memorable. Most years, the display of autumn foliage in northwestern Connecticut is the equal of any in New England, beginning with September's golden days, when purple asters and goldenrod bloom beside country roads, and reaching a climax in mid-October, when the brilliant red maples and golden beech and hickories stand out against the deep green of the hemlocks. Then the hills are covered with a rich tapestry of colors that are reflected in the mirror surface of each pond and lake.

SHARON AUDUBON CENTER

At the Sharon Audubon Center, a sanctuary of the National Audubon Society, old stone walls speak of the land's early use for farming. Today, the center's 684 acres offer a rich and varied environment for wildlife—fields, woodlands, two ponds, streams, and marshes that are home to many species of birds and such mammals as beaver, otter, mink, red and gray foxes, deer, bobcats, squirrels, and rabbits.

In the main building, you will find a bookstore and gift shop, a museum, the Hal Borland Room, and a children's discovery room. The museum displays focus on the birds, mammals, insects, and reptiles native to Connecticut.

The Hal Borland Room, a memorial to one of New England's best-loved nature writers, contains photos, a collection of the author's books, and even his manual Remington typewriter. It was in the fall of 1941 that Borland's first outdoor essay appeared in the *New York Times*. In the ensuing years he wrote some 1,200 more. A selection of these essays was published in 1964 under the title *Sundial of the Seasons*. Borland's other books about nature include *An American Year*; *This Hill, This Valley*; *The Enduring Pattern*; and *Beyond Your Doorstep*.

Although Borland was born in Nebraska and spent much of his boyhood on a homestead in eastern Colorado, during much of his adult life he lived with his wife, Barbara, in a country house in Salisbury, Connecticut, on the Housatonic River. From his observations of this hill and valley country in northwestern Connecticut, he drew the inspiration for his books and essays about the natural world.

The Sharon Audubon Center has a Hal Borland Trail, .75 mile long, which begins near the native wildflower garden and continues through brushland and deciduous forest to a streamside hemlock forest.

What came to my mind on that warm, perfect May day of sunshine, spring flowers, and new growth everywhere was the chapter on woodlands in *Beyond Your Doorstep*. Borland writes that to find an abundance of spring wildflowers, one should seek out a patch of deciduous woodland on a slope facing southeast. Here the plants can grow in the deep leaf mold and receive the sunlight they need from mid-October until mid-May. Most of these early spring wildflowers blossom and then die back before summer's canopy of leaves shuts out the sunlight. About fifty-five species of wildflowers bloom in the area during March, April, and May. May is the time to look for the pink and yellow lady's slippers, blue wood violets, and jack-in-the-pulpits amid flowering dogwood.

In the gift shop and bookstore, I picked up a trail map and guide to the sanctuary grounds and eleven miles of trails. Near the main building is the native wildflower garden, where Virginia bluebells, columbine, and white violets were in bloom. The garden was planted and is maintained by the Sharon Garden Club.

Beginning near the parking area is a short trail that is

**Grebes are small diving and swimming birds
that need an expanse of open water to take flight**

wheelchair accessible. Known as the Lucy Harvey Multiple Use Interpretive Area, it was designed by the Housatonic Audubon Society in cooperation with the National Audubon Society for use by "the elderly, the very young, the disabled, and short walk enthusiasts."

I walked Fern Trail, a narrow, rocky woodland trail, one mile long, that follows the northern shore of Ford Pond. On this day in May, the pond reflected the sky and all the pastel shades of the spring foliage. A pair of Canada geese and their downy young swam near the shore. I learned that a great blue heron, a brown creeper, and a golden-crowned kinglet were recently sighted near the pond and that over seventy species of birds were seen on a spring bird walk on sanctuary grounds. As I walked wooded Fern Trail, I found many varieties of ferns, such as Christmas and cinnamon ferns, and wildflowers too. Blue and yellow violets brightened the spring woods.

The Hendrickson Bog Meadow Trail is a loop walk of 1.6 miles through deciduous woodlands and along the edge of Bog Meadow Pond, where you may see signs of beaver activity. You pass through a lovely high meadow with a few cedar, white birch, and white pine trees. From there I walked through a stand of pine to the shore of Bog Meadow Pond. Surrounded by wetlands and hills on the farther shore, this pond offers a feeling of remoteness. I sat under a huge maple on the shore and watched for wildlife. Red-winged blackbirds called from the marshes, and the surrounding woods were filled with birdsong.

Other trails to explore are Ford Trail, 1.6 miles through deciduous and hemlock forest; Hazelnut Trail, a short loop trail one mile long; and Woodchuck Trail, 2.35 miles through open fields and deciduous forest, which gives you a great view to the west. After a morning walk on the trails, you can enjoy a picnic lunch at tables on the lawn near the main building.

Part of the work of the center involves maintaining an injured and orphaned wildlife rehabilitation program. Primarily, birds are cared for here. Mammals and reptiles are referred to other local wildlife rehabilitators. Visitors can view a display on bird rehabilitation. As many as 150 birds may be cared for during a given year. Birds that have been cared for at the center include an American kestrel with a broken wing and a red-tailed hawk suffering from a gunshot wound.

While it is sick or injured birds that are most often brought to the center, during the severe winter of 1993–94, the Sharon Audubon Center suddenly found itself playing host to horned grebes that had become stranded in northwestern Connecticut. Grebes are small diving and swimming water birds. In all, there are twenty-six species, six of which are found in North America. Those seen in Connecticut usually migrate from their summer range in northwestern Canada to the Atlantic Coast to spend the winter. Along the coast and in lakes and estuaries, they feed on small fish, shrimp and other crustaceans, and insects. That winter, because of the severe cold, grebes that strayed inland found all bodies of water frozen. Mistaking dark, wet roads and parking lots for open water, they landed on them in search of food. Needing an expanse of open water from which to take flight, these birds found themselves stranded. Over the course of the winter, a total of seven horned grebes were fortunate to be rescued by caring persons who took them to the Sharon Audubon Center. Here they were content to swim in the library bathtub and feed on minnows. Each consumed a dozen or more every day. After a checkup and their fill of fish, the grebes were driven to Grass Island in Greenwich, Connecticut, and released into Long Island Sound. Those who work in the wildlife rehabilitation program say that the most satisfying part of their work is being able to release a bird back into the wild.

Two separate buildings at the center house the educational facilities for the Northeast Region of the National Audubon Society. An educational program brings more than 5,000 schoolchildren to the Sharon Audubon Center each year. Summer environmental programs for different age groups are also offered, as well as a series of weekend environmental programs for adults and children. Spring programs include an Owl Prowl and Wood-cock Walk in March, a Beaver Walk and a Wildlife Rehabilita-tion Workshop in April, and an Amphibian Walk in May.

Where: Two miles southeast of Sharon on State 4.

Hours: Grounds open daily, dawn to dusk, year-round. The center is open Monday to Saturday 9:00 A.M. to 5:00 P.M. and Sunday 1:00 to 5:00 P.M.

Admission: A small fee is charged for admission to the grounds and trails. No additional charge for attending most weekend en-vironmental programs. Fees vary for the summer environmental programs for children. Those who join Friends of the Sharon Audubon Center receive free admission to the center and trails as well as other discounts.

Best time to visit: Spring to see wildflowers; otherwise, any sea-son of the year is a good time. An insect repellent will come in handy during the spring months to discourage blackflies.

Activities: Bird- and wildlife watching, hiking, wildflower garden, photography, picnicking, cross-country skiing, snow-shoeing, and environmental programs for adults and children, including classes, workshops, walks, and special events.

For more information:

Sharon Audubon Center, National Audubon Society, 325 Cornwall Bridge Road, Sharon, CT 06069; 203-364-0520 (Mon-day to Friday 9:00 A.M. to 5:00 P.M.).

MACEDONIA BROOK STATE PARK

Located in Kent, in mountainous terrain near the New York State border, Macedonia Brook is one of Connecticut's largest state parks, notable for its unspoiled natural beauty, miles of hiking trails, abundant woodland bird species, and large natural campsites. Macedonia Brook with its deep gorge and waterfalls crosses the park. Some of the most appealing campsites are along the brook. Especially during spring and fall bird migrations, this is one of the best places in the state to camp and enjoy early-morning bird walks.

Established in 1918 with a gift of 1,552 acres from the White Memorial Foundation, the park now encompasses 2,300 acres and two mountain peaks, including Cobble Mountain, the highest point at 1,380 feet. The Connecticut Blue Trail crosses Cobble Mountain and several other peaks, from which you get fine views of the Catskill and Taconic Mountains in New York. Numerous streams add to the pleasure of hiking in this park. For a spectacular view of the gorge of Macedonia Brook, stop near the park entrance, where the remains of a forge operated by the Kent Iron Company in the mid-1800s is located. The forge was a stamping works that required vast amounts of charcoal, which led to the destruction of the original forests by 1848.

Visiting the park today, you detect little hint of the region's early history as a center of industry. In fact, the huge maples along the park road seem always to have been part of the landscape. I first visited this park some years ago on a beautiful October day. With the abundance of maple trees, the woods were a symphony of color. After eating lunch at a sunny picnic table, I hiked the park road that follows Macedonia Brook, enjoying the bright foliage, the crisp crunch of dry leaves underfoot, and the sound of the swiftly flowing brook.

A trail map is available from the park office. You can climb the trail to the summit of Cobble Mountain or follow any one of a number of less strenuous loop trails. Most of the trails start from the park road. In general, those to the east of the road are less steep than the trails to the west.

Also available from the park office is a map of the portion of the Appalachian Trail that passes through northwestern

Connecticut. Part of the trail has been relocated so that it no longer passes through Macedonia Brook State Park. However, you can gain access to the AT from State 341, just south of the park. The old segment of the AT that passes through the park is now part of the Blue Trail system.

This is one park that doesn't seem to be overcrowded even on summer weekends. On a clear, warm Sunday in late August, I found plenty of campsites available and uncrowded trails for hiking. The eighty-four spacious sites are grouped in four separate campgrounds. In addition to the sites along Macedonia Brook in Hickory Campground, you can choose from Birch Campground and, farther along the park road, Overlook and Maple Campgrounds. My favorite site is tucked away in Upper Birch Campground on a hillside beneath a huge white pine. Facilities include fireplaces, water from an old-fashioned pump, and outhouses. It's a good idea to bring an insect repellent, because blackflies linger in these forests even as late as August.

Like the campsites, the picnic sites are spread out over a large area. A large stone and wood picnic pavilion can be used by groups or for shelter on rainy days. Some camp and picnic sites, including the pavilion, are accessible to the handicapped.

The ranger on duty that August day reported seeing quail, white-tailed deer, and raccoons in the park. Ruffed grouse are common, and many hawks had also been observed that morning. Later, from a picnic site, I watched a red-tailed hawk soaring over the park and heard its high-pitched scream. This large, common hawk with a wingspan of forty-eight inches has a whitish breast and rust-colored tail. It prefers deciduous forests with adjacent open country and feeds mainly on small rodents.

This is also a fine area to see woodland bird species, especially during the spring and fall migrations. In May the trees may be filled with warblers moving through the park. Species that nest in the area include black-and-white, blue-winged, black-throated blue, and golden-winged warblers. Other songbirds that nest in these woods are thrushes, winter wrens, scarlet tanagers, and rose-breasted grosbeaks.

In spring, anglers come to this park to enjoy stream fishing. Macedonia Brook is annually stocked with trout. Along with the opportunity to see birds, spring camping provides the possibility of having pan-fried brook trout for breakfast!

In winter, this is a good park for cross-country skiing. This area of northwestern Connecticut often has snow cover even when the ground is bare elsewhere in the state. Check with the park office before you go for information on which trails are suitable for skiing.

Where: Four miles north of Kent off State 341.

Hours: Open for day use from 8:00 A.M. to sunset daily, year-round, as conditions permit. Campgrounds open from April 16 through September 30. Check with the park office first if you are planning to camp before Memorial Day or after Labor Day. Also, one campground may be kept open after September 30 for late-fall camping.

Admission: No charge for day use. A daily fee is charged for camping.

Best time to visit: During spring and fall migrations to see record numbers of birds. Otherwise, any season is a good time to enjoy this park.

Activities: Hiking, bird-watching, camping, stream fishing, picnicking, and cross-country skiing. No ranger-led activities, but rangers are available during the summer season to answer questions. Trail maps are available at the park office.

Concessions: None.

Pets: Pets are not allowed in campgrounds or near streams.

For more information:

Macedonia Brook State Park, 159 Macedonia Brook Road, Kent, CT 06757; campground office, 203-927-4100; park office, 203-927-3238.

KENT FALLS STATE PARK

Three miles north of Kent on US 7 in the Litchfield Hills is one of my favorite state parks and one of Connecticut's most dramatic waterfalls. Kent Falls State Park, which covers 275 acres, was a gift to the state in 1919 by the White Memorial Foundation. The falls, formed by the waters of Falls Brook, drop eighty feet in the upper cascade, which must be reached by foot, while a series of lesser falls over steep rocky slopes and ledges of white marble bring the total drop to 200 feet. The falls are most spectacular in the spring, when the volume of water is greatest, but, for me, it is the sight of the lower falls framed by October's brilliant colors that comes to mind. Surrounded by the bright gold of the hickories, the crimson leaves of the maple trees, and the dark green of the hemlocks, the cascading water is an unforgettable sight that attracts photographers as well as those who enjoy hiking, fishing, or a picnic.

While there is no swimming in the park, wading in the pool at the base of the lower falls is a good way to cool off on a hot day. Children can explore for hours in and around the small pools of the brook, and stream fishermen can enjoy fly-casting for trout.

The picnic area is spread out through the park and has some choice tables with a view of the falls as well as some large secluded picnic sites that were at one time campsites.

I have visited this park many times and seldom drive by it without stopping, but one time that I especially remember is the early October day when two friends and I hiked the trail to the upper falls. What started out as an impromptu picnic turned into a real feast, for Angela, Mary, and I lingered a long time, enjoying the food, the warm sun, the fall foliage, and the splendid view of the falls.

It was midafternoon by the time we approached the rustic staired pathway, constructed by the Youth Conservation Corps, that leads to the upper falls. A forest of hemlocks clings to the steep hillside and shelters a garden of ferns and mosses. Looking down, we had a fine view of the gorge carved through the rock walls by the force of water. We found potholes where the swirling water had worn away the softer layers of rock. Here and there, a side trail leads to the rocky gorge, where you'll find sunlit pools of water and close-up views of the cascading waters of the upper falls. We were enveloped in the cool and quiet of the forest, where the only sounds were those of falling water and the call of a chickadee. Climbing higher, we reached the top of the falls, where the water, surrounded by a halo of golden leaves, caught the sunlight. The view from here is well worth the climb. Often when the cold rains of November or the ice storms of January or February keep me inside, I recall that sunny, golden day spent in the hills of northwestern Connecticut.

Spring, summer, and fall are all good times to visit. While it may be crowded on a summer weekend, the ample parking and well-spaced picnic sites provide room for one more person or family to enjoy this park.

Where: Three miles north of Kent on US 7.

Hours: From 8:00 A.M. to sunset daily.

Admission: Entrance fee on weekends and holidays from April 15 through the end of September.

Best time to visit: Spring or fall for viewing the falls or hiking. Spring for fishing. Any season to enjoy a picnic. Bring insect repellent, as blackflies may be present even in late summer.

Activities: Picnicking, fishing, hiking, and photography. No ranger-led activities are offered.

Concessions: None. However, you may often find an ice-cream vendor in the parking area on summer weekends.

Pets: Permitted on a leash in the picnic area. Not allowed near the falls or brook.

Facilities: Free parking, picnic tables, rest rooms, and drinking water. Facilities accessible to the handicapped include the parking area, picnic tables, and a telephone.

For more information:

Bureau of Parks and Forests, Connecticut Department of Environmental Protection, 79 Elm Street, P.O. Box 5066, Hartford, CT 06106-5066; 203-566-2305.

LAKE WARAMAUG STATE PARK

Surely Lake Waramaug, surrounded by forests and the Litchfield Hills, is one of Connecticut's most prized lakes. Located in Kent and New Preston, it has been compared to Switzerland's Lake Lucerne, and few bodies of water in the state can rival its splendor when the bright hues of autumn are reflected in its blue depths. At the head of the lake, Lake Waramaug State Park occupies ninety-five acres along the west shore. It's one of my favorite destinations for camping, swimming, picnicking, and canoeing.

Lake Waramaug was named for the chief of the Wyantenock Indians, who once used the area as their hunting grounds. The park is part of some 4,000 acres of land within the geographical boundaries of the town of Kent that have been set aside as parks or public lands. Macedonia Brook and Kent Falls are the other state parks. Together they preserve some of Connecticut's finest natural areas.

Kent's early settlers, however, viewed the wilderness as an enemy to be conquered. The town became the center of an early ironmaking industry. On the grounds of the Sloane-Stanley Museum are the remains of an old iron-smelting furnace of the Kent Iron Company, which was in operation from 1826 to 1896. The furnaces used charcoal as fuel, and thousands of trees were cut for the charcoal kilns. Others were taken for lumber to build houses, leaving the hills bare and ugly. The iron industry has been gone for almost a hundred years, time enough for a fine second-growth forest to make the hills lush and green again.

In summer, Lake Waramaug State Park is a prime destination for swimming and a picnic, or perhaps an afternoon of canoeing along the park's undeveloped west shore. From Memorial Day through Labor Day weekend, North American Canoe Tours rents canoes and pedal boats. While canoeing or walking along the shore, you are almost certain to see a flock of Canada geese. The clear water and sand beach make for enjoyable swimming, and shaded picnic tables overlooking the lake provide a cool place to eat lunch.

Lake Waramaug State Park also has one of Connecticut's most attractive campgrounds, with eighty-eight well-spaced sites in a grassy, shaded area overlooking the lake. Services include a food concession and modern rest rooms with showers. You may camp here from May 15 to September 30.

For spectacular scenery, most would agree that the best time to visit this park is mid-October, when the trees lining the lake shore turn to brilliant shades of red and gold. I remember one bright October day when my friend Katherine and I followed the narrow, winding shore road, nine miles in length, that encircles the lake. It is best to do this on a weekday when traffic is light, and you can give your undivided attention to the views of water and foliage that unfold at every turn in the road.

In winter, the lake's frozen surface becomes a great place for an afternoon of ice skating. You may want to combine a winter outing with a fireside dinner or Sunday brunch at the Inn on Lake Waramaug, located near the state park at 107 North Shore Road in New Preston. It is one of the area's charming country inns that attract visitors year-round.

Where: Five miles north of New Preston off State 45 on Lake Waramaug Road.

Hours: Open for day use from 8:00 A.M. to sunset daily. The campground is open from May 15 to September 30. Campsites are available for rental until 10:00 P.M. each evening.

Admission: There is a day-use fee weekends and holidays from Memorial Day through Labor Day weekend. Campers pay a nightly fee per campsite.

Best time to visit: Weekdays in summer for swimming, canoeing, and camping. Advance reservations for campsites are advisable during the summer season. Try spring or fall for uncrowded camping. Mid-October is usually the best time for fall foliage viewing.

Activities: A Camper Nature Program is offered in the summer, with rangers on duty during the camping season. Swimming, picnicking, camping, canoeing, fishing, scuba diving, hiking, and ice skating. There are handicapped-accessible facilities for camping and picnicking, including a picnic shelter.

Concessions: A food concession is open during the summer season. Also during the summer, canoes and pedal boats are rented by North American Canoe Tours, Inc., 65 Black Point Toad, Niantic, CT 06357; 203-739-0791 (off-season 813-695-4666).

Pets: Not permitted.

For more information:

Lake Waramaug State Park, 30 Lake Waramaug Road, New Preston, CT 06777; campground office: 203-868-0220; off-season information number, 203-868-2592.

Applications for campsite reservations must be received at least ten days in advance. They are accepted by mail beginning January 15 and should be sent directly to the campground.

MOUNT TOM STATE PARK

On a bright, windy, cool day that was more like October than early September, I drove to Mount Tom State Park, located off

US 202, west of the center of Litchfield. This 233-acre park is memorable for its fine sand beach, excellent swimming, waterfront picnic sites, and the Tower Trail, which affords a marvelous view from the crest of Mount Tom.

The park has tables and fireplaces, bathhouses, rest rooms, and a food concession. Drinking water is available from a hand pump.

The major portion of the park was donated by Charles H. Sneff and his wife, Gustavia, in 1911. It is believed to be the first gift to the state of land valued mainly for its great natural beauty.

The sixty-two-acre pond is largely spring-fed with clear, deep water. Development is limited to some private cottages on the opposite shore. Because no motors are permitted on the pond, it is a good place for canoes. You can also launch a car-top fishing boat or small sailboat. The pond is stocked with trout.

On hot summer days, the beach area may be crowded, but with many other picnic tables scattered in wooded areas of the park, you can usually find a quiet spot for yourself even on summer weekends.

An off-season visit has its own advantages. On that September day, while eating lunch and drinking a welcome cup of hot coffee, I watched two brave girls go swimming! They declared the water to be "nice and invigorating." Another bonus, they had the sand beach and swimming area all to themselves! In the off-season, also, the marshy area on the opposite shore of the pond is a good place to observe waterfowl. I saw black ducks and mallards that day.

Behind the waterfront area, on the wooded hillside, you will find the beginning of the 1.5-mile Tower Trail, which follows a moderately steep gravel road. In spring, the white blossoms of shadbush light up the woods. As you hike, look for the characteristic rectangular holes drilled by the pileated woodpecker. They are usually found on dying trees that have been invaded by colonies of black carpenter ants. Especially in winter, these birds

Feeding their hungry nestlings is a full-time job for pileated woodpeckers

may actually help save the life of a tree by feeding on the ants until the colony is destroyed, enabling the tree to recover. If you're lucky, you may catch a glimpse of this spectacular crow-sized woodpecker, with its bright red crest, or hear the sound of its drilling echoing through the woods. This bird usually builds its nest in the tall stub of a dead tree, in dense forest, well hidden by the surrounding leafy branches of live trees.

The trail ends at the summit of Mount Tom (at an elevation of 1,325 feet), near a stone tower that is thirty-four feet high. From the roof of the tower, a marvelous view of Mount Tom Pond is spread out before you far below. To the northwest is the Riga Plateau, and to the right are Bantam Lake and the white church spires of Litchfield. If the day is really clear, you can even see Long Island Sound to the south.

The round-trip hike takes only about an hour, but, of course, you will want time to spend on the summit enjoying the view; and combining the hike with swimming or canoeing and a picnic makes for an ideal day in the outdoors.

Where: Seven and a half miles west of Litchfield off US 202. Look for the "State Park" sign on the left after passing a view of Mount Tom Pond.

Hours: 8:00 A.M. to sunset daily, year-round, as conditions permit.

Admission: Parking fee Memorial Day through Labor Day weekend.

Best time to visit: Spring and fall for hiking and boating. Summer for swimming. Bring insect repellent to discourage black-flies in spring and early summer.

Activities: Swimming, scuba diving, picnicking, fishing, canoeing, sailing, hiking, fall foliage viewing, ice skating.

Concessions: A food concession is in operation during the summer months and weekends in the fall, featuring such fare as hamburgers and hot dogs, chili, ice cream, soft drinks, and coffee.

Pets: Not allowed on the beach. Pets on a leash are permitted on the Tower Trail.

Other: Camping is available nearby at the White Memorial Foundation's two campgrounds and at two private campgrounds: Hemlock Hill Camp Resort, P.O. Box 828, Hemlock Hill Road, Litchfield, CT 06759 (203-567-2267), and Looking Glass Hill Campground, P.O. Box 1610, Litchfield, CT 06759 (203-567-2050).

For more information:

Bureau of Parks and Forests, Connecticut Department of Environmental Protection, 79 Elm Street, P.O. Box 5066, Hartford, CT 06106-5066; 203-566-2305.

WHITE MEMORIAL FOUNDATION AND CONSERVATION CENTER

The largest wildlife refuge in Connecticut, the White Memorial Foundation consists of some 4,000 acres of woodland, open fields, ponds, marshland, and Bantam Lake shore property in the towns of Litchfield and Morris. This natural treasure owes its existence to the foresight and generosity of two local residents, Alan C. White and his sister, May W. White. Feeling that the lake and surrounding countryside should be preserved for the public to enjoy, the Whites, between 1908 and 1912, purchased several large tracts of land, extending north and east of Bantam Lake. In 1913, they conveyed the land as the White Memorial Foundation, Inc. In addition to the gift of land, the Whites added an endowment to help with the cost of development and maintenance of the property. The White Memorial Conservation Center houses a Nature Museum and one of the finest nature libraries in the state.

A wide range of facilities for outdoor study and recreation includes thirty-five miles of beautifully maintained trails, campgrounds, boating facilities, meetinghouses, and special areas for large indoor gatherings.

Nature Museum

Before attempting to explore any of the trails, visit the Nature Museum and adjacent bookstore and gift shop, where you can purchase an excellent trail map for $2.00.

The museum features changing exhibits and dioramas depicting the wildlife of the area at different seasons of the year. An exhibit of mounted specimens of Connecticut owls lets you take a close look at the great horned owl, screech owl, barred owl, saw-whet owl, snowy owl, short-eared owl, and long-eared owl, which is an endangered species in Connecticut. The great horned owl, barred owl, and screech owl all breed in the forests of the refuge. Other exhibits in the museum focus on the wild turkey, which has been successfully reintroduced into Connecticut; mammals found in Connecticut; and Connecticut hawks. Live turtles, including a box turtle and a painted turtle, are part of a wetlands exhibit, which tells us that these areas are among the most productive on earth in terms of biological diversity.

Another exhibit provides information about Catlin Woods — the near-climax forest of oaks, birches, hemlocks, and occasional large white pines — which is part of the foundation's lands. Catlin Woods is one of the four tracts of land that have been established as strict natural areas for scientific and educational purposes. Although you may explore these areas on established foot trails, the land is being maintained as free as possible from human interference, allowing only natural forces to bring about change. Catlin Woods is a good place to look for warblers, thrushes, and owls.

Nature Trail

On a bright, warm day in mid-September, I hiked the self-guiding Nature Trail that begins near the museum. It is an easy trail to hike, about one-half mile long, with seventeen marked stations, which are interpreted in a guide you can purchase for a small fee in the museum store.

The start of the trail is lined with tall sugar maples. To the right is an open field that is used for activities, but it is also home to birds and animals that live in open spaces. Looking closely, you may see a woodchuck, cottontail rabbit, or wild turkey. A spreading oak tree often produces a large crop of acorns, providing food for the squirrels, wild turkeys, wood ducks, and blue jays that inhabit the refuge. The trail passes through a white-pine forest and then turns left toward the Bantam River.

From the forest, I emerged into a marsh area where grasses, sedges, and shrubs provide food and shelter for many species of wildlife. Ducks, great blue herons, rails, marsh wrens, swamp sparrows, and red-winged blackbirds are often seen here and in other open marsh areas. To the right of the marsh, near the river, I found the shrubs filled with songbirds—chickadees, white-breasted nuthatches, eastern phoebes, and several species of warblers that I found hard to identify as they flew from branch to branch or were concealed by the dense shrubbery.

The portion of the trail that follows the Bantam River is a special delight. Here I watched a flock of black ducks. On another day, I watched a canoeist paddle the slow-moving river, which meanders through the northern half of the White Memorial Foundation. A canoe trip is an ideal way to look for waterfowl and wading birds that frequent the river and surrounding wetlands. River otters are occasionally seen. If you own a canoe, by all means bring it with you.

From the river the trail turns left, and I found myself in an old-growth forest. A large pine, well over 200 years old and three feet in diameter, towered 100 feet above the forest floor. Most of the smaller trees are eastern hemlock, which are very tolerant of shade. As I walked, I noticed depressions and mounds on the forest floor. These signify that it is an old forest. Many of the low areas were created when trees, now long gone, became uprooted, leaving hollows in the earth. The mounds were formed by the long-since-decayed root masses of the big trees.

Looking down, I noticed the evergreen plants growing on the forest floor: goldthread, shining club moss, and partridge berries. In the soft, wet mud of a low area I also found deer tracks. And I also discovered a number of owl pellets beneath a tree. If you can locate an owl's feeding roost, you have a good chance of seeing the bird if you return to the woods after dark.

Holbrook Bird Observatory

Back at the parking area, I picked up my lunch and headed for one of the picnic tables near the Holbrook Bird Observatory. The observatory, which has thirty sheltered viewing stations available for bird-watchers and photographers, overlooks an area land-scaped with shrubs that attract a variety of birds in all seasons. A bird-feeding station is filled with food during the winter months. With the aid of a pair of binoculars, you can combine eating lunch with bird-watching.

Lake Trail

During the afternoon, I hiked the Lake Trail, which is one mile in length and leads to a bird-observation platform overlooking Bantam Lake. I walked past fields of goldenrod and purple asters before entering the North Bay Natural Area, which includes the wetland habitats at the north end of Bantam Lake's North Bay. The most common trees in the swamp are red maples. This swamp is home to water thrushes, grouse, vireos, yellowthroats, woodpeckers, and nuthatches.

Nearer the shore of the lake where the soil is dry for at least part of the summer is an area of high willows. To the north is a ridge composed of lake-bottom mud and rocks, fashioned over the years by the winter forces of nature, which cause the water to freeze, then expand and contract, producing great pressure on the bottom of the lake. The vegetation on this ridge is quite different from that in the surrounding swamp. In addition to red maple, I saw ash, elm, black willow, and red oak. At the edge of the lake is a thick growth of buttonbush, which flourishes in the shallow water.

Emerging from the swamp to the bird-observation platform was one of my most memorable moments while exploring White Memorial Foundation trails. From the platform, I had a mar- velous view of North Bay and the marsh areas along the shore. Since it was mid-September and not a weekend, there was little human activity, and I felt as if I had reached the shore of a wilderness lake. Such an impression is rare, because during the summer there is considerable activity on Bantam Lake, the largest natural lake in Connecticut. Nevertheless, on this bright, clear afternoon, only one or two motorboats broke the stillness as I watched a flock of black ducks feeding in the marshes and several herring gulls flying overhead. Then I was surprised to see a double-crested cormorant—a rare sight in these inland waters—land on a concrete pier. The bird-observation platform was built in 1972 on the concrete piers of an old railroad that extended into the lake and was used when ice was harvested and shipped to New York City.

On the return hike, I came across some closed gentians

growing with the goldenrod beside the trail. It has been years since I have seen these in the wild. With their deep blue blossoms, they are among the loveliest wildflowers we have in Connecticut.

Some 165 different species of wildflowers grow on White Memorial Foundation lands. May is probably the most exciting month to see wildflowers. Fifty-six different species bloom during this month, including such beauties as white and painted trillium and the lovely pink lady's slipper known as the moccasin flower.

Mattatuck Trail

Part of the Mattatuck Trail, one of Connecticut's best hiking trails, passes through White Memorial Foundation lands. The thirty-five-mile-long trail starts at Mad River Road in Wolcott and crosses Prospect and Mohawk Mountains before joining the Appalachian Trail in Cornwall. If you hike the 6.2-mile segment of the trail that passes through the refuge, you will have an introduction to all of the refuge's varied habitats except the shore of Bantam Lake. Species of wildlife that you may see include water thrushes and ducks at Beaver Pond; duck broods and swallows at Fawn Pond; and beaver, along with flycatchers and warblers, at Heron Pond. (The Heron Pond Trail, which is .6 mile in length, circles the pond and connects with the Mattatuck Trail.) The Mattatuck Trail then passes near Cranberry Pond, a good place to look for herons. Both the great blue and the green-backed heron nest in the refuge.

After passing through Catlin Woods, the trail crosses the Bantam River and intersects with the Pine Island Trail near the Duck Pond. As its name implies, the Duck Pond is another good area to look for nesting ducks in the spring. Those nesting in the refuge include mallards, American black ducks, blue-winged teal, wood ducks, and hooded mergansers.

Little Pond Trail

Accessible from South Lake Street, Little Pond Trail includes a boardwalk that provides access to a wetland area frequented by herons, swallows, and ducks. In 1985, Hurricane Gloria caused significant damage to the original boardwalk. During the past nine years, a White Memorial crew has rebuilt the boardwalk. The project was completed in August 1994.

Camping

You will have an even better opportunity to see birds and other wildlife if you camp at one of the foundation's family campgrounds.

Point Folly has forty-seven sites on a peninsula that extends into Bantam Lake. The waterfront campsites are the kind you dream about on winter evenings. Tenting and trailer RV camping are allowed. The size of the trailer permitted depends on the site involved and is subject to the approval of the camp manager. Drinking water, pit toilets, and a dumping station are provided. Not provided are hookups for recreational vehicles, showers, or a shelter. A campground store and marina are located near the entrance to Point Folly. Public boat-launching facilities are available at the marina. Sandy Beach, located on Bantam Lake, can be used by campers for a nominal fee. The campground at Point Folly opens in early May and closes on Columbus Day.

The other campground, Windmill Hill, has twenty large sites shaded by pine, oak, and maple trees. Open from Memorial Day weekend through Labor Day, it is restricted to tent camping. In late September, when I walked through the campground, the only sounds I heard were the chatter of a pair of red squirrels and chickadees calling from the branches of the pine trees. In late fall, Windmill Hill is a good place to look for winter birds, including kinglets and, occasionally, pine grosbeaks.

Reservations for campsites are advisable and are accepted by mail only until Memorial Day weekend. After that, make your reservation in person at the campground store. Telephone reservations are not accepted. The minimum reservation is two days and three days on holiday weekends. The maximum stay is fourteen days. All sites not reserved in advance are available on a first-come, first-served basis.

Both of these campgrounds are designed to offer a quiet, unspoiled camping experience and access to the wonders of nature to be found in the refuge.

I can't imagine a better inland area for birding in Connecticut than the White Memorial Foundation. As of the fall of 1993, a total of 246 species had been reported on foundation lands. Information in the foundation's *Guide to Birding* includes the times of the year species are seen, an indication of their abundance, and a record of those that nest in the refuge. Just to give you an idea of the wealth of bird life in the refuge, the list of breeding birds includes the ruby-throated hummingbird, pileated woodpecker, red-bellied woodpecker, great crested flycatcher, winter wren, eastern bluebird, blue-gray gnatcatcher, golden-crowned kinglet, many species of warblers, northern oriole, scarlet tanager, rose-breasted grosbeak, and the rare indigo bunting.

Camping at the White Memorial Foundation also provides the best opportunity to catch a glimpse of some of the mammals that make their home within the refuge, especially since many of these are active mainly at night. Commonly seen are red and gray squirrels, chipmunks, woodchucks, white-tailed deer, eastern coyotes, raccoons, and eastern cottontails. Seven species of bats have been seen in the refuge, with the little brown bat being the most common.

Less-often-seen species include mink, which prefer forested, log-strewn areas near streams and marshes. Muskrat are occa-

Eastern bluebirds nest in tree cavities, old woodpecker holes, fence posts, and bluebird boxes

sionally seen from the boardwalk around Little Pond. Weasels and even the rare fisher, which prefers dense hardwood-softwood forests, have been seen. The foundation's wetlands are also home to the river otter, a playful animal that enjoys sliding down steep banks. Even the bobcat, rare in Connecticut, has been spotted by museum staff, and during the summer of 1993 a black bear was seen passing through the refuge in the Point Folly area.

Cross-Country Skiing

In the winter, when there is snow, about thirty-five miles of trails are open for cross-country skiing and snowshoeing. Snowmobiles and all-terrain vehicles are not allowed. The trails, which are not groomed, are open to the public seven days a week. Most of the trails are relatively flat, but several are challenging, an attraction for more experienced skiers. No trail fee is charged. Trail maps may be purchased at the museum store. The activity shed, located behind the museum, is open to skiers and is equipped with picnic tables and a woodstove. Outhouses are the only rest rooms provided.

Periodically during the winter, interpretive nature walks on skis are held on weekends. These are free to the public. Brief reports of snow depth and conditions may be obtained by calling the museum at 203-567-0857.

Where: The entrance to the White Memorial Foundation and Conservation Center is located about two miles west of Litchfield, off US 202 on Whitehall Road.

Hours: The grounds are open daily twenty-four hours. The Conservation Center, which houses the Nature Museum, library, and bookstore, is open Tuesday through Saturday 9:00 A.M. to 5:00 P.M., Sunday 11:00 A.M. to 5:00 P.M. April through October. For the rest of the year, the center is open Tuesday through Saturday 8:30 A.M. to 4:30 P.M., Sunday 11:00 A.M. to 4:30 P.M. Closed January 1, Easter Sunday, July 4, Thanksgiving (including the Friday after Thanksgiving), and December 25. Library hours: Tuesday through Sunday 2:00 to 4:30 P.M. The foundation office is open Monday through Friday 7:30 A.M. to 4:30 P.M.

Admission: No charge for use of the trails and roads for hiking, nature study, horseback riding on designated roads, or cross-country skiing. Weekend walks and programs are also free of charge. However, many families and individuals choose to become members of the White Memorial Foundation in order to help support the foundation's goals in education, conservation, research, and recreation. A small fee is charged for admission to the museum. Campers pay a nightly camping fee. There is also a charge for having visitors at your campsite.

Best time to visit: Each season is special: spring for nesting birds and wildflowers, summer for camping and canoeing, autumn for fall bird migrations and the splendor of fall foliage in the Litchfield Hills, winter for cross-country skiing and looking for animal tracks and winter birds. Spring, summer, and fall are good for hiking, nature study, and horseback riding.

Activities: Hiking, picnicking, horseback riding, camping, canoeing, fishing for northern pike and bass, cross-country skiing, bicycling, bird-watching, orienteering, and weekend nature walks and other programs.

Horses are allowed on designated woods roads and other roads throughout the refuge as shown on the White Memorial Guide Map. Horse-trailer parking is allowed along the edges of the Activity Field and Sawmill Field.

There is no place to rent a canoe in the immediate area, but Main Stream Canoe Corp. in New Hartford (203-379-6657) and River-running Expeditions Ltd. in Falls Village (203-824-5579) do offer rentals.

Rentals of cross-country ski equipment are available from the Wilderness Shop in Litchfield (203-567-5905).

Concessions: None.

Pets: Pets on a leash are allowed. If you are camping with your dog, it must be confined on a leash not more than seven feet in length, and you must stay with your pet at all times.

Other: Several publications, including the trail map, checklists for birds and wildflowers, and a guide to the Nature Trail, are available at the museum store. A section of the foundation property has been mapped for the increasingly popular sport of orienteering. There is also a complete range of facilities for group use, including the Carriage House with dormitories; dining and meeting facilities; and the Mott–Van Winkle Classroom, which is fully equipped and available for year-round group programs, with seating for seventy-five persons, blackboards, and audio-visual facilities.

For more information:

White Memorial Foundation and Conservation Center, P.O. Box 368, 71 Whitehall Road, Litchfield, CT 06759; 203-567-0857.

TOPSMEAD STATE FOREST

Hidden away off Buell Road in Litchfield is a very special place – Topsmead State Forest. Topsmead is the former summer home of Edith M. Chase of Waterbury, daughter of Henry S. Chase, the first president of the Chase Brass Company of Waterbury. Designed by famed architect Richard Henry Dana Jr., the Tudor-style "cottage" was completed in 1924. It is situated atop a 1,230-foot-high knoll from which you have a wonderful view out over the surrounding countryside to the distant hills. Flower gardens, rolling lawns, well-kept pastures, hayfields bordered by beautiful stone walls, and forestland are all part of the property. During her lifetime, Miss Chase, who was a former director of the Connecticut Forest and Park Association, was fond of roaming the fields and woods of her summer home. She liked to observe the many species of birds and wildflowers she found there. From the natural world she drew a sense of renewal that enabled her to face again the challenges of the business world.

When Edith Chase died in 1972, she left Topsmead, which includes the summer home and 514 acres of land, to the people of Connecticut. It was her desire that Topsmead be managed to protect its natural beauty, allowing passive and casual recreational pursuits such as hiking, picnicking, nature study, cross-country skiing, and snowshoeing.

In planning for the future of the area, the Department of Environmental Protection called for development of a forty-acre wildflower preserve and a nature trail, which were constructed during the summers of 1974 and 1975 by the Connecticut Conservation Corps and dedicated to Edith M. Chase.

A right turn off Buell Road leads to the entrance to the parking area. Nearby you can pick up a trail map. The Edith Chase Ecology Trail and wildflower preserve are just north of the parking area. Look for the trail sign to the right of the small pond. This area of wooded wetlands is also an excellent site for observing songbirds, especially along the pond outlet brook. The northeast corner of the preserve has a natural small marsh that attracts plants and birds found only in a wetland habitat. The preserve is home to over 200 plant species, including abundant wildflowers and ferns.

While spring is the best time to get your fill of wildflowers in bloom and also to observe nesting songbirds, the trail is worth walking at other seasons of the year as well. In early September, I heard the familiar calls of chickadees, nuthatches, and phoebes. In the groves of tall hemlocks, sunlight barely filtered through the dark branches, but the stands of swamp maple were already displaying a reddish tinge. Various trees and shrubs that provide food for wildlife have been added to provide a more diverse habitat. I observed squirrels and chipmunks busy with the task of storing a winter's food supply, and I heard, from deep in the marsh, the musical "ker-r-r-r-ock" of a leopard frog.

A picnic table near the pond is a good place to stop for lunch. Blue and white asters and feathery goldenrod were in bloom that September day, and the sweet smell of freshly cut hay filled the late-summer air. A short distance into the woods from the pond, you can duck into a rustic bird blind, constructed with wooden benches, a perfect spot for observing birds and other wildlife without being seen.

Interpretive plaques erected by the Boy Scouts along the nature trail contain much information that will add to your understanding of the relationships between organisms and their environment. One sign, entitled "The Pyramid of Life," explains that the foundation of life is soil, which along with sunlight and rain produces plant life. All animals, including man, depend on plants directly or indirectly for energy. It concludes, "Man should know that all life depends on the soil; as the soil goes, so goes all life."

Back at the parking lot, I picked up my lunch and walked up the road to the Tudor-style cottage. Magnificent tall pines and hemlocks line the road. On this clear, warm afternoon, the view out over the surrounding countryside was impressive. Topsmead, built of masonry and cypress with a slate roof, contains most of its original furnishings. It is open to the public during the summer and fall on designated days. From here you have a choice of several miles of hiking and cross-country ski trails, roads, and open fields that invite exploration.

Horseback riding is permitted on certain trails, and I followed one that led between high fields bordered by handsome stone walls. When you live in a wooded valley as I do, you really appreciate being in this wide-open country where you can see for miles. Monarchs and spangled fritillaries glided over the fields, stopping to feed on the goldenrod and asters that blossomed by the side of the road. On the way back, I caught my breath as an eastern bluebird flew across the field and perched on a branch in a large pine tree. This was an exciting moment because it had been years since I had seen a bluebird in Connecticut. The population of this once-common bird declined due to the use of insecticides, competition from other birds such as starlings, and the disappearance of the old orchards that were its favorite nest sites.

Not only is there an orchard at Topsmead, but nesting boxes have been erected in the fields to provide additional sites. Bluebirds feed on a varied diet that includes grasshoppers, beetles, flying insects, and caterpillars, as well as berries and other fruit.

You'll find picnic tables placed at inviting sites, but you are also encouraged to spread your blanket out and enjoy your lunch wherever you choose. Picnic fires are not permitted. One family had come by bicycle and was having a picnic in the shade of a huge maple. A group of horseback riders passed along the trail. An artist was setting up his easel, and a young woman had come in search of a quiet place to read.

While hiking at Topsmead, you may see white-tailed deer. Look for them feeding in the fields at the edge of the woods early in the morning or toward dusk. The orchard, when there are apples on the ground, is another likely spot. In the winter, you can sometimes follow deer tracks on skis or snowshoes. During severe winter storms, they often gather in dense stands of evergreens, especially hemlocks, which are a favorite winter food. After a fresh snowstorm, you can find their bedding spots in these sheltered areas.

In the high fields or near the brushy edges of woods, you may see woodchucks. They are daytime animals. Clover and alfalfa are favorite foods, but they eat a variety of plants, not to mention cultivated vegetables if they can find such gourmet fare. A shrill whistle is their cry of alarm.

You will probably not see raccoons, which are active mainly at night. Should you see one, a park sign warns visitors not to approach this animal because of its susceptibility to rabies, which has now spread from the mid-Atlantic region into most areas of Connecticut.

One of the plaques along the nature trail gives the following prescription for survival: "Man in balance with nature in a peaceful world." Walking the trails at Topsmead, one feels that here, at least, that vision has been achieved.

Where: From the intersection of State 63 and 118 in the center of Litchfield, drive two miles east on State 118. Turn right on East Litchfield Road. In one-half mile, turn right onto Buell Road.

Hours: The state forest is open daily from 8:00 A.M. until dusk, year-round as conditions permit. The Topsmead "cottage" is open weekends and holidays, noon to 5:00 P.M. June through October, on the second and fourth weekends of the month.

Admission: Free to the public.

Best time to visit: Anytime during the year: spring for wildflowers and nesting songbirds, autumn for fall foliage walks, and winter for cross-country skiing.

Activities: Hiking, bird-watching and nature study, picnicking, horseback riding, cross-country skiing, snowshoeing, and sledding. Tours of the Chase summer home.

Concessions: None.

Pets: Permitted on a leash.

Other: Trail maps are available at an information station near the parking area. However, except when the house is open to the public, there is generally no ranger on duty to answer questions about the trails or wildlife.

For more information:

Bureau of Parks and Forests, Connecticut Department of Environmental Protection, 79 Elm Street, P.O. Box 5066, Hartford, CT 06106-5066; 203-566-2305.

FLANDERS NATURE CENTER

Flanders Nature Center in Woodbury is a wonderful place to observe wildlife or simply to enjoy an afternoon hike on well-marked and maintained trails. A drive of about ten miles north from I-84 in Southbury transports you into another world, where land is managed for the benefit of wildlife as well as man and where traffic and shopping malls seem very far away.

Flanders Nature Center was founded in 1963 by the late Natalie Van Vleck. The center is an educational organization as well as a land trust, with holdings in Woodbury, Bethlehem, Middlebury, and Southbury.

The office and sanctuary headquarters and most of the trails are located at the Van Vleck Farm Sanctuary on Flanders and Church Hill Roads in Woodbury. Stop at the farmhouse office and obtain a trail map before driving up Church Hill Road to the parking area. You are welcome to bring a picnic lunch as long as you carry out any refuse.

Trails on the north side of Church Hill Road take you to the sanctuary's varied habitats: a pond; woodlands, including a

Woodchucks are likely to be out and about in daytime

nut-tree arboretum; fields; wetlands; and the farm's pumpkin patch, site of a popular fall program that offers a hayride to the pumpkin patch to choose a pumpkin and listen to an educational discussion about pumpkins.

On a late summer day as I started along the Wildlife Habitat Trail, the woods were cool, a welcome refuge from the sun. From a wooden bench placed in a good position for pond viewing, I watched painted turtles sunning themselves on a log. The pond draws many other species of wildlife. In the fall, migrating ducks stop to feed and rest. Farther along the trail, I stopped to watch a great blue heron. Standing in shallow water near the shore, the bird remained motionless for nearly ten minutes before suddenly lowering its long neck and head into the pond and catching a fish. Then, with its struggling prey held securely, the heron spread its great wings and flew off across the pond. This is one method the heron uses for fishing. The other is to carefully stalk its prey as it moves along the edges of the pond in shallow water. When a frog or fish is sighted, the heron strikes quickly with its sharp beak. The heron's diet also includes insects and mice.

In addition to the pond, other sources of food attract wildlife. Fruit-bearing shrubs grow along the banks. Farther down the trail, nut trees tempt small mammals, and fields attract seed-eating birds. Not only is there food here, but shelter is also provided—even nesting boxes for wood ducks supplement the natural sites. The only sounds I heard were the calls of chickadees, catbirds, and a nuthatch and the chattering of a red squirrel.

The Botany and Wildlife Luncheon Trails are on the south side of Church Hill Road. Plan to hike the Botany Trail during the month of May when many of the more than 100 species of wildflowers are in bloom. The trail, created in 1965, is maintained by members of the Pomperaug Valley Garden Club of Woodbury. In addition to flowers, you will find nineteen species of native ferns along this trail, plus nine species that have been introduced to the area. Be sure to look for the dark green fronds of the abundant Christmas ferns and the delicate fronds of the maidenhair ferns.

Bordering Botany Trail is Flanders Tree Farm, an eye-pleasing plantation of white spruce, scotch pine, and blue spruce, which are being managed as Christmas trees. Bluebird nesting boxes have been placed among the spruce trees. However, providing suitable nesting sites is only half the battle in aiding the eastern bluebird. The nesting-box program had a frustrating season in 1993. Predators such as sparrows and raccoons killed some of the baby birds, and house wrens, throughout the nesting season, attempted to take over the boxes. Removing the wren nests and installing baffle devices to prevent raccoons from getting to the nests helped, but at the end of the nesting season, only ten of the twenty-six babies hatched had survived to become fledglings. However, the 1994 season was highly successful, with twenty-five fledglings raised and no losses.

During 1993 and 1994, a new program was developed at Flanders that features organic gardening, an in-the-barn classroom, and farm animals. The goal was to create a model farm space for plants, animals, and people. Under the guidance of John Clark, a local gardener, volunteers helped manage the garden while learning about soil enrichment, plant lore, insect identification and appreciation, and composting. Volunteers also worked on a barn complex and learned about the care and handling of domestic animals. Through the Farm and Garden Program, visitors can now learn about low-impact gardening, protection of water quality, and soil conservation, as well as the care of farm animals.

Throughout the year, to enhance understanding and appreciation of the natural world, Flanders Nature Center offers many other programs for children and adults, from guided walks to an annual Ecology Day in August.

During the month of March, you can visit Flanders's maple-syrup house on Cowles Road in Woodbury, learn about the history of maple-syrup making, and watch syrup being made in the traditional way.

The annual Fall Festival weekend is held the first weekend in October, with activities for families, hayrides, games, and refreshments.

During July and August, Flanders offers nature classes at a summer day camp for children ages four to twelve. Brochures for registration are available from the office in May.

In winter, bring your cross-country skis or snowshoes to explore the sanctuary's trails and look for animal tracks and other signs of winter wildlife.

Where: To reach the sanctuary headquarters in Woodbury, drive north on US 6, seven miles from exit 15 on I-84. Flanders Road is the second left after the intersection of State 47 and 132 (Main Street). Watch for the farmhouse and "Nature Center" sign on your right at the intersection of Flanders and Church Hill Roads.

Hours: Flanders Nature Center is open daily from dawn to dusk year-round. The office is open Monday to Saturday 9:00 A.M. to 5:00 P.M.

Admission: Admission to the trails at the Van Vleck Farm and Whittemore Sanctuaries is free. Those who become members of Flanders Nature Center and Land Trust receive special discounts and the center's quarterly newsletter.

Best time to visit: Spring to see wildflowers, March to learn how maple syrup is made; but each season is special at Flanders, and any time is a good time to visit.

Activities: Nature study, photography, hiking, picnicking (no fires), cross-country skiing, and special programs.

Pets: Not allowed.

For more information:

Flanders Nature Center, P.O. Box 702, Woodbury, CT 06798; 203-263-3711.

2

Southwestern Connecticut

In a lifetime of seeing beauty in the wilderness,
I always feel a lift of spirit and an afterglow
of serenity and content.
I also know one must take time and wait
for the glimpses of beauty that always come,
and one must see each as though
it were his last chance.

— Sigurd F. Olson
Reflections from the North Country

In southwestern Connecticut, where I have lived for thirty years, I have received many unforgettable "glimpses of beauty." Although you will not find any true wilderness areas in this part of the state, it offers many beautiful places and special wild locales where plants, birds, and other wildlife flourish.

What I remember best is the autumn foliage reflected in the mirror surface of Squantz Pond, the sight of a great blue heron feeding in a shallow area of the pond at Southford Falls State Park, the joy of glimpsing a pair of Baltimore orioles in spring at the Ansonia Nature and Recreation Center, and the combination of wild roses, dunes, and piping plovers on a sparkling morning in June at the Smith-Hubbell Wildlife Sanctuary.

Depending on what interests you in nature, may you build your own store of enduring memories as you explore the special places of southwestern Connecticut.

SQUANTZ POND STATE PARK

Surrounded by steep wooded hills, Squantz Pond State Park, four miles north of New Fairfield, is one of Connecticut's prettiest parks, especially in the fall, when the red and gold foliage of the maples and oaks is reflected in the pond's mirror surface. The pond is named for the chief of the Pootatuck Indians who once used this area as their hunting grounds. Some years ago, a well-preserved Indian war canoe was discovered at the bottom of the pond.

In 1926, the state purchased 173 acres for the park. Land for Pootatuck State Forest, which is adjacent to the park, was acquired by the state between 1926 and 1928, thus protecting from development the entire western shore of Squantz Pond.

A natural spring-fed body of water, Squantz Pond is an arm of Candlewood Lake, one of the largest artificial bodies of water in the Northeast. The lake was created in 1926 as a power reservoir into which water from the Housatonic River is pumped from the Connecticut Light and Power Company's Rocky River Hydraulic Plant in New Milford.

Although I have visited Squantz Pond State Park several times, what stands out in my memory is one Indian-summer day in late October. Having driven to the town of Sherman near Connecticut's western border, I headed south on State 39, which follows the eastern shore of Squantz Pond. At every turn in the road, the views of the foliage and the clear blue water of the pond were spectacular.

When I reached the park, I found only a few other cars in the parking area. The sight of the long sandy beach and boat-launching area evoked memories of summers past. Squantz Pond has one of the state's most attractive swimming beaches, the surrounding hills creating the impression that you are beside a mountain lake. During the summer months, you can rent a canoe; and although the beach may be crowded on summer weekends, paddling along the pond's undeveloped western shore is still a pleasant experience.

Fall and spring are ideal for canoeing, although you must bring your own canoe with you then. I remember wishing that my canoe was not in New Hampshire, for that Indian-summer day, with little wind, warm sun, and the display of brilliant color, would have been perfect for paddling.

The picnic area has tables and fireplaces. I had lunch at a sunny table overlooking the pond. The hills were a patchwork of red, orange, gold, and green, which contrasted with the bright blue water of the pond.

The hiking trails are on the west side of the pond. The main trail, known as the Lake Trail, is about two miles long and begins at the north end of the picnic area. I hiked this trail, which descends a hill, crosses a rustic bridge over a stream, and follows along the western shore of Squantz Pond. Here the forest reaches to the water's edge, and a rocky ridge rises from the shore of the pond to a height of more than 400 feet. An old guidebook indicates that a trail up this steep hillside led to the Council Rock of the Pootatucks and an adjoining cave. Actually, there are many caves on state-forest land and side trails leading away from the pond that can be explored. The main trail crosses two more streams before it curves to the right and ends at a small peninsula from which you get a fine view of the entire pond.

The park is a good area for seeing woodland songbirds and small mammals such as woodchucks, rabbits, red and gray squirrels, and chipmunks. The deep forests were once home to the lynx, which today in the East is found only in northern New England and extreme northern New York State. However, the rocky hills still provide sanctuary for the bobcat, which gets its name from its stubby tail.

The waters of Squantz Pond and adjoining Candlewood Lake are stocked with trout each year, so fishermen find a good supply of brown and rainbow trout as well as largemouth bass and yellow and white perch.

Squantz Pond is also one of Connecticut's parks where you can engage in winter activities. When the temperature dips well below freezing, the smooth surface of the pond provides excellent ice skating; or you may choose to spend a day in the park cross-country skiing or hiking on snowshoes.

Where: Four miles north of New Fairfield on State 39.
Hours: Open from 8:00 A.M. to sunset daily.
Admission: Parking fee during the summer season and on weekends from April 15 through Memorial Day and from Labor Day through the end of September.

THE ELUSIVE BOBCAT

Now rare in Connecticut, the bobcat is seldom seen. A nocturnal animal, it spends its days in some safe hiding place such as a rock cave or thicket where its mottled fur provides good camouflage. It is also an excellent climber. A low tree branch often serves as an observation post from which it can watch for a rabbit or mouse to pass by and provide a meal. The bobcat mates in the spring when a rock shelter, fallen tree, or hollow log may serve as the protected place it seeks for its den.

Best time to visit: Spring and fall for hiking and quiet canoe trips. Summer for swimming, picnics, and canoeing. (Rental canoes are available.) To avoid crowds, visit the park on a weekday. Winter for ice skating and cross-country skiing.

Activities: Swimming, scuba diving, hiking, picnicking, fishing, boating, cross-country skiing, and ice skating. Facilities include a boat-launching ramp, modern rest rooms, a first-aid station, and drinking water.

Concessions: A food concession is in operation during the summer months. In addition, during the summer season, canoes and pedal boats are rented from North American Canoe Tours, Inc., 65 Black Point Road, Niantic, CT 06357; 203-739-0791 (off-season, 813-695-4666).

Pets: Not allowed on the beach or near the pond. Pets on a leash allowed on wooded trails.

For more information:

Bureau of Parks and Forests, Connecticut Department of Environmental Protection, 79 Elm Street, P.O. Box 5066, Hartford, CT 06106-5066; 203-566-2305.

SOUTHFORD FALLS STATE PARK

Located off State 188 in Oxford, Southford Falls State Park is an easily accessible park that is fun to visit at any season of the year. Waterfalls on the Eight Mile River, a pond that attracts waterfowl, and the possibility of seeing nesting bluebirds in the spring are just three of the reasons to visit this park.

At the turn of the century, the park was the site of the Diamond Match Company. The land, which encompasses 120 acres, was acquired by the state in 1932 after a fire destroyed the factory buildings.

On a cool, sunny day, the first weekend in October, I found the leaves just beginning to take on their autumn colors, and the pond was framed by delicate shades of red and gold foliage. Today, the name of the pond (Papermill Pond) is one of the few reminders that this was once an industrial site. Now the pond with its water plants and marshes is a haven for waterfowl. On this October day, a great blue heron was feeding in a shallow area near shore and a small flock of Canada geese was moving toward the center of the pond. The melodious honking of flocks of wild geese heading south is one sound that I always associate with autumn in New England.

The circular hiking trail skirts the shore of Papermill Pond past a wildlife marsh to an overlook. The most memorable stretch of the trail follows the Eight Mile River with its cascading falls through a deep, hemlock-lined, rocky gorge to a covered bridge. From the falls, it is just a short walk back to the parking area.

Many come to this park to fish for trout along the banks of the Eight Mile River. Kids often fish the river from the bridge near the parking area. Also near the parking lot are handicapped-accessible picnic and fishing areas. Other facilities include a picnic and warming shelter, rest rooms, and drinking water. Picnic sites with grills overlook the pond and the falls, making Southford Falls a favorite spot for families to come for a Sunday afternoon picnic.

On a spring bird walk, you may see nesting wood ducks in the pond; and among the returning songbirds, you can have the thrill of seeing the rare eastern bluebird. Nesting boxes have been set on poles, eight to twelve feet above the ground in open areas. They are helping to compensate for the widespread destruction of the old apple orchards that provided this bird's favorite nesting sites.

The park is usually uncrowded, so if you are not seeking a place to swim, boat, or camp, it is a peaceful haven where you can spend a summer day by a rushing stream or among cool hemlock woods.

In winter, the park is open for ice skating, ice fishing, sledding, cross-country skiing, and snowshoeing. The park's location on a state road makes it easy to reach even in winter. It is a good place to look for winter birds or to follow animal tracks after a fresh fall of snow. The tracks of white-tailed deer, cottontail rabbits, opossums, raccoons, gray and red squirrels, and ruffed grouse are commonly seen in the winter woods.

Where: One-half mile south on State 188 from the intersection of State 67 and 188 in the village of Southford.
Hours: 8:00 A.M. to sunset, daily, as conditions permit.
Admission: None.
Best time to visit: This park is not overly crowded, so any season is a good time to visit.
Activities: Hiking, picnicking, and fishing. In winter, sledding, cross-country skiing, snowshoeing, and ice fishing.
Concessions: None.
Pets: Allowed on a leash on trails and in the picnic area.
For more information:
Bureau of Parks and Forests, Connecticut Department of Environmental Protection, 79 Elm Street, P.O. Box 5066, Hartford, CT 06106-5066; 203-566-2305.

KETTLETOWN STATE PARK

Located five miles south of Southbury, Kettletown State Park takes its name from the fact that early settlers in this area purchased a large tract of land from the Indians in exchange for one brass kettle. The park extends for about two miles along the eastern shore of Lake Zoar. The lake was created by the damming of the Housatonic River when Stevenson Dam was constructed for the purpose of obtaining hydroelectric power.

Well-spaced campsites, a sandy swimming beach, several

marked hiking trails, and a Camper Nature Program during the summer months make this park a good destination for a weekend or a vacation.

The seventy-two partly wooded and open campsites are situated in three separate areas. When I visited the park on the first Sunday in October, only a few campers were taking advantage of the near-perfect fall weather. Doubtless, rain the previous evening had sent some of the weekend campers home. One camping area has sites in a grassy, hilly area partially shaded by maples and spruce trees. Another offers shaded sites among hemlock, oak, maple, and black-birch trees.

Camping facilities include flush toilets, showers, and a dumping station. There is an outdoor amphitheater used for nature programs and a separate campers' recreation area. Campers are allowed to use the Campground Recreation Area Shore to launch carry-in boats. Boat trailers are not allowed in the park. Trailers and RVs are limited to twenty-six feet in length.

The swimming beach and picnic area are located in a cove of Lake Zoar. Paugussett State Forest, which extends along the opposite shore, is a large undeveloped area for hiking, fishing, and nature study. The lake offers fishing for largemouth and smallmouth bass as well as white and yellow perch.

The Pomperaug Trail is located entirely within Kettletown State Park except for the southern end at the Jackson Cove Recreation Area. By combining this trail with the Crest Trail, a loop trip of 3.8 miles is possible. The best time to hike this trail is in June when the groves of mountain laurel are in bloom. The views of Lake Zoar are also a reason to hike this trail.

You can hike the Oxford Loop of the Pomperaug Trail as a continuation of the main trail or as a separate short hike of 1.55 miles. Parking is available at the Jackson Cove Recreation Area. The trail crosses Mill Brook, once the site of a factory that made cedar chests and other furniture. Old roads in this area descending toward the lake are a reminder that this valley was once a farming community before the construction of Stevenson Dam. Small rock caves and a waterfall on Mill Brook are two noteworthy features of this trail.

The Miller Trail, another loop of 1.55 miles, is in the northwestern section of the park, accessible from the picnic-area loop road. The trail ascends to an overlook for a bird's-eye view of Lake Zoar.

The entrance to the handicapped-accessible nature trail is off the campground road. Along this short loop trail, as well as other trails within the park, are good areas to look for woodland birds — species such as chickadees, woodpeckers, rose-breasted grosbeaks, warblers, thrushes, nuthatches, woodland flycatchers, and scarlet tanagers. Early morning and late afternoon until dusk are the best times to observe bird activity.

Where: Five miles south of Southbury, exit 15 off I-84. South on Kettletown Road for four miles, then right on George's Hill Road.

Hours: Open for day use from 8:00 A.M. to sunset daily. The campground is open from mid-April through Columbus Day. Campsites are available for rental until 10:00 each evening.

Admission: Fee for day use on weekends and holidays from Memorial Day through Labor Day weekend. There is also a nightly camping fee.

Best time to visit: The park is busiest in summer, when reservations for campsites are advisable. Spring and fall are the best times for hiking, nature study, and quiet camping.

Activities: A Camper Nature Program is offered in the summer. Swimming, hiking, camping, fishing, picnicking, nature trail, and field sports. Camping, picnicking, nature trail, and field sports are handicapped accessible. Carry-in boats such as canoes may be launched by campers from the Campground Recreation Area Shore. Boat trailers not allowed in the park.

Concessions: None. Food services, laundry, etc., are available along Main Street in Southbury.

Pets: Not allowed in the campground, beach, or lake areas. Pets on a leash are permitted on hiking trails and in designated picnic areas.

For more information:

For trail maps and information off-season: Bureau of Parks and Forests, Connecticut Department of Environmental Protection, 79 Elm Street, P.O. Box 5066, Hartford, CT 06106-5066; 203-566-2305.

For information during the camping season: Kettletown State Park, Southbury, CT 06488; campground office, 203-264-5678; park office, 203-264-5169.

Applications for reservations are accepted, by mail only, beginning January 15 and must be received at least ten days in advance of the intended reservation period. Camping-permit applications must be mailed directly to the campground.

FARMINGTON CANAL LINEAR PARK
AND LOCK 12 HISTORICAL PARK

In Connecticut and elsewhere, a new type of park is being created. It is known as a linear park or greenway. In contrast to most traditional parks, linear parks are narrow belts of open space that may stretch for many miles. The recently completed segment of Farmington Canal Linear Park in Cheshire, which opened in May 1994, is an example of this type of park.

In Connecticut, the plan to transform abandoned railroad corridors and former canals into trails for hiking, bicycle riding, and open-space conservation is giving new life to the historic Farmington Canal.

THE HISTORY OF THE FARMINGTON CANAL

The idea to build the canal dates back to January 29, 1822, when businessmen from New Haven met with representatives from sixteen other towns. Lacking the trade advantage that the Connecticut River gave to Hartford and mindful of the success of New York State's Erie Canal, they proposed building the Farmington Canal, which they envisioned as eventually connecting the St. Lawrence River with Long Island Sound. Work was started near the Massachusetts border on July 4, 1825. Engineered by Henry Farnum under the direction of James Hillhouse and Eli Whitney, the canal opened in 1828. The section that was completed ran from New Haven Harbor through Hamden, Cheshire, Southington, Plainville, Farmington, Avon, Simsbury, and Granby (all in Connecticut) to Northampton, Massachusetts, a total of eighty-three miles, making it the longest canal in New England. The work of building the ten-foot-wide towpath and the four-foot-deep channel for the canal, which was regulated by twenty-eight locks to accommodate the 213-foot rise between New Haven and the Massachusetts state line, was all accomplished by men working with draft animals and simple scoops and drags. The work also involved the construction of an aqueduct over the Farmington River.

For almost twenty years canalboats carried both freight and passengers along the waterway. However, frequent landslides made the cost of maintenance very high, resulting each year in losses for the stockholders, until in 1847 operations were suspended. In 1848, the canal was replaced by a railroad that remained in operation until 1982, when floods washed out part of the line in Cheshire.

In 1980 Cheshire restored a section of the old canal, making it Lock 12 Historical Park. Located off State 42, the park consists of the towpath beside the canal, the lock, the lockkeeper's house, a helicoidal bridge, a museum, and a picnic area.

Today the portion of the canal line that passes through Cheshire is once again serving as an avenue of transportation. Instead of canalboats, today's travelers go on foot, bicycle, or

roller skates. The paved trail extends for 2.8 miles from Cornwall Avenue to Mount Sanford Road. Access to Farmington
Canal Linear Park is near the restored lock, or you can pick up
the trail where it crosses State 42.

Walking the trail on a weekday in early May, I found white
dogwood, apple, and cherry trees in bloom. As the trail traverses
an area of wetlands, I listened to the calls of frogs and red-
winged blackbirds and, at one point, saw ripples in the water and
the nose of an animal that was quite possibly a muskrat. From the
leafy branches of tall trees came a medley of birdsong. I spotted
many robins and catbirds among the returning songbirds, as well
as year-round residents like cardinals, woodpeckers, nuthatches,
and blue jays. Heading north toward Cornwall Avenue, I found
mallard ducks swimming where canalboats once traveled. Houses
and backyards are often visible, but along other portions of the
trail, you can gaze across a hillside pasture or perhaps stop to
wonder at the great variety of life in the extensive wetlands.
Once an avenue of commerce, the linear park, which is maintained by the Cheshire Parks and Recreation Department, now
provides area residents with a close-to-home opportunity to
enjoy the outdoors.

Cheshire's Farmington Canal Linear Park is part of the
Farmington Canal Heritage Trail, which, when all the towns involved have completed restoration work along the canal bed, will
link New Haven, Connecticut, with Northampton, Massachusetts, via a pathway eighty miles long, extending nearly the entire
length of the canal.

South of Cheshire, the town of Hamden, after completing
design work for its northern three-mile section of the trail, began
construction on the path in October 1994. The project should be
finished by August 1995. New Haven has acquired a 2.1-mile
section of the canal that runs through the Yale University campus
and Science Park and plans to begin cleaning up the canal bed so
that it can be used for hiking and biking. In the northern part of

the state, from Farmington to Granby, six towns are working to develop twenty-five miles of the trail.

Building the Farmington Canal Heritage Trail is a goal that encourages land preservation, historic preservation, and alternative means of transportation while at the same time benefiting everyone with increased opportunities for hiking, cross-country skiing, birding, and nature study. The trail will also benefit wildlife by helping to link together tracts of land that have already been set aside for refuges and parks.

Where: From the center of Cheshire, go south two miles on State 10. Turn right on State 42 (North Brooksvale Road). Lock 12 Historical Park and parking area will be on your left.
Hours: Lock 12 Historical Park is open March through November, daily 10:00 A.M. to 5:00 P.M. The museum is open at special times and by appointment. Tours with costumed guides are scheduled in the spring and fall. Call for information.

Farmington Canal Linear Park is open daily, sunrise to sunset.
Admission: Admission is free to both Lock 12 Historical Park and the Farmington Canal Linear Park Trail.
Best time to visit: Any time is a good time to follow this trail, but birders and nature-study enthusiasts will find early-morning hours and weekdays less crowded. Because this is a multiuse trail, it is very popular with bicyclists and in-line skaters. However, even on a Sunday afternoon during the 4th of July weekend, there seemed to be room for all—young and old—to enjoy the trail in their own way.
Activities: Hiking, jogging, bicycling, roller skating, bird-watching, cross-country skiing, in addition to touring the historic lock and enjoying lunch in the picnic area of Lock 12 Historical Park. The canal trail is wheelchair accessible and is also ideally suited for pushing young children in strollers. Prohibited on the trail are motorized vehicles (except wheelchairs), horses, and skateboards.

Pets: Dogs on a leash are allowed.

For more information:

Lock 12 Historical Park, 487 North Brooksvale Road, Cheshire, CT 06410; 203-272-2743.

Cheshire Parks and Recreation Department, 559 South Main Street, Cheshire, CT 06410; 203-272-2743.

Connecticut Trust for Historic Preservation, 940 Whitney Avenue, Hamden, CT 06517; 203-562-6312.

ANSONIA NATURE AND RECREATION CENTER

The citizens of Ansonia can be proud of their nature center. It is one of only two nature centers that serve the towns of the Naugatuck Valley. The other is the Kellog Environmental Center in Derby. Situated on 104 acres that encompass fields, woods, a fishing pond, and a swamp, the Ansonia Nature and Recreation Center has two and a half miles of trails. With such diverse habitats, it is home to many species of wildlife. A walk on these trails can be a fascinating experience at any season of the year.

The nature-center building houses a nature museum, displays on local environmental issues, a small nature library, a gift shop, and space for programs.

In front of the main building are native fern and wildflower gardens and a butterfly garden that attracts hummingbirds as well as butterflies. In mid-May, yellow violets and red trillium were in bloom. If I had come a week later, I could have seen the blossoms of the yellow lady's slipper.

The Ansonia Nature and Recreation Center is an ideal place for families with young children because it also has a marvelous home-grown playground built by the community. In addition, there are athletic fields, a picnic grove, two covered picnic pavilions, and community gardens.

Executive director of the center Donna Lindgren is a

licensed wildlife rehabilitator. Under her direction and with the help of a small staff and volunteers, the Ansonia Nature Center is playing an increasingly important role as a rehabilitation facility for orphaned and injured birds and animals. In 1993, about 450 birds and animals were cared for. The goal is to be able to release the bird or animal back into the wild. During the past ten years, the center has nursed many species of birds back to health, including a turkey vulture, owls, and kestrels. When I was at the center in May 1994, four baby screech owls had been brought there for care. Injured squirrels and rabbits have also been cared for at the center. Those interested in wildlife are anxious to help an injured or orphaned bird or animal. However, removing a bird or animal from its natural surroundings is a drastic step that may not have a happy ending. If the creature is injured, there may be little choice, but if you find a baby bird or animal alone, chances are good that the parent is nearby and will return to care for its offspring if you don't interfere.

In the nature-center building, you can pick up a trail map that shows the primary circular nature trail and the network of secondary trails that connect to it. I followed the main trail down the slope toward the tranquil pond. A side trail on the right proved to be an excellent area to see robins, mockingbirds, blue jays, and a pair of Baltimore orioles. Lindgren said that the orioles were nesting at the nature center and that scarlet tanagers had nested there the previous season. An indigo bunting has also been sighted in the area, as well as migrating warblers.

When I reached the pond, where several children were fishing, I heard the call of a red-winged blackbird from a marsh, and I watched a pair of swallows swooping low over the pond. Crossing a bridge, the trail follows the edge of a field before entering a forested area. Swallows had appropriated several of the bluebird nesting boxes set out in the field. Red cedars, maples, wildflowers, and ferns grow in the wooded area. A sudden shower cut short my walk, but on the way back I stopped, despite the rain, to watch a cottontail rabbit continuing to nibble fresh blades of grass and clover, undisturbed by my presence.

In speaking about birds seen at the center, Lindgren expressed concern that neotropical migrants (birds such as warblers, swallows, vireos, and robins that each year travel to and from South America) are in deep trouble due to the destruction of habitat through overdevelopment in both the United States and South America. Each year fewer migratory warblers and wood thrushes are seen in Connecticut, and the song of the meadowlark is seldom heard these days.

It is thought that the key to preventing further decline in our songbird population lies in managing large natural areas in a way that makes them attractive to birds. Linear parks, which link together smaller parks and preserves, can also help to combat the fragmentation of the landscape caused by overdevelopment, which may be as damaging to migrating birds as the destruction of the tropical rain forests in South America.

Chuck Collinge, an outdoor writer and part-time ranger at the Ansonia Nature Center, told me about other wildlife that might be seen while walking the trails. Wild turkeys, pheasants, woodcocks, and ruffed grouse are attracted to the area. An authority on wild turkeys, Collinge, who has written the book *Nutmeg Turkeys: A Guide to Wild Turkeys in Connecticut*, advised that if you get out early in the morning, just after dawn, you have a better chance of seeing the birds. White-tailed deer and woodchucks are also seen by visitors.

Throughout the year, the Ansonia Nature and Recreation Center sponsors a number of programs, field trips, and bird and wildflower walks. In addition, children can attend a program of natural-history classes during the month of July.

Where: From the intersection of State 115 and 243 in Ansonia, follow 243 east. Turn left (north) on Benz Street (by Warsaw Park). Bear right on Milan Road to Deerfield Lane.

Hours: The park is open daily, dawn to dusk, year-round. The nature-center building is open daily year-round, except on major holidays, from 9:00 A.M. to 5:00 P.M.

Admission: No admission charge, but visitors may wish to join the Friends of the Ansonia Nature Center to help support the center's programs.

Best time to visit: Spring to see birds and wildflowers; fall for foliage walks and to see migrating birds; winter for cross-country skiing; summer for nature walks and picnics.

Activities: Bird-watching, wildflower walks, nature photography, hiking, fishing, playground and athletic fields, picnicking, cross-country skiing, displays and special programs: films, nature walks, and natural-history classes for children. A calendar of events is available. Camping is by special permit only, in designated areas.

Bicycles, horses, snowmobiles, and other motorized vehicles are not allowed on the trails.

Pets: All pets must be on a leash.

For more information:

Ansonia Nature and Recreation Center, 10 Deerfield Lane, Ansonia, CT 06401; 203-736-9360.

SMITH-HUBBELL WILDLIFE SANCTUARY

One of the best areas in Connecticut to see shore and water birds is the Smith-Hubbell Wildlife Sanctuary located at Milford Point in the town of Milford. Over 230 species of birds have been recorded in the area, making this 8.7-acre sanctuary, which is managed by the Connecticut Audubon Society, a favorite destination of bird-watchers since the 1930s. In a heavily populated section of the southwestern coast of Connecticut, it is indeed fortunate that this area of marsh at the mouth of the Housatonic River and beach on Long Island Sound has been preserved for wildlife.

When I visited the sanctuary in the spring of 1994, a restoration project sponsored by the Connecticut Audubon Society, the New Haven Bird Club, and the Department of Environmental Protection was nearly complete. The land is owned by the state of Connecticut and leased by the Connecticut Audubon Society. The project called for the construction of a boardwalk over the low dune area to the beach, and benches on the boardwalk provide a wonderful spot to sit and scan the edge of the tide and the offshore barrier beaches for birds. The restoration effort has also involved the removal of invasive plant species and the replanting of native species designed to provide an improved habitat for wildlife. The planting of wild roses, which were in bloom in

**Plovers scattered along the edge of the waves
search for food to bring back to their beachfront nests**

early June, not only aids wildlife but has transformed a rather barren area into a place of beauty.

Smith-Hubbell is a sanctuary for two of Connecticut's threatened species of birds—the piping plover and the least tern. Fencing helps protect the low dune area, the nesting ground of the piping plover, a pale sand-colored bird with orange legs and a black, yellow-tipped bill. A single neckband also helps identify this bird. Arriving in March, the birds seek an isolated sandy beach with sparse vegetation for their nesting grounds. They must also have access to mudflats for feeding. In late April, the first eggs are laid in a shallow depression in the sand, often lined with shell fragments and placed near vegetation. The three or four eggs, which are cream-colored with dark brown flecks, hatch in twenty-seven days. The chicks leave the nest within hours of hatching and are very vulnerable to beach traffic and predators. As I watched several adult plovers feeding at the edge of the tide, I heard their whistled call of "peep-lo."

The least tern is a gull-like bird about the size of a robin. The long pointed wings have a span of about twenty inches, and the tail is forked. It has a gray back, white belly, white forehead with a black cap, black wingtips, and yellow feet and bill. Arriving in early May, least terns form pairs that stay together the whole season. They prefer broad, sandy, vegetation-free beaches located close to an estuary with an abundant supply of food. Here the two small offshore barrier beaches serve as the nesting grounds for the least terns. In mid-May, the first eggs are laid in a shallow depression in the sand. The nests have one to three cream-colored eggs with dark brown blotches. The eggs hatch in twenty-one days, and the young leave the nest by the second day. By the twenty-third day, they are able to fly but continue to be fed by the parents until migration.

Several factors have led to the decline in numbers of both these species in Connecticut. Shoreline development has limited the availability of suitable nesting sites, and beach-stabilization projects have reduced the quality of the remaining sites. The birds are forced to use areas with more vegetation, which gives cover to predators like dogs, cats, rats, raccoons, and skunks. Human disturbance, which can include outright nest destruction, is also a factor. When visiting the refuge—or any beach area—during nesting season, from April 1 to September 1, it is extremely important to keep away from the nesting areas. Disturbing the birds prevents them from attending to their nests and young. If dogs are allowed on the beach, they should be kept on a leash at all times. In addition, food scraps that might attract predators should not be left on the beach.

From the parking area on the other side of Milford Point, you have a good view of the extensive marshes that are part of the Charles E. Wheeler Preserve. In June, I saw great and snowy egrets in the marsh and killdeer feeding on the mudflats. Great blue and green herons as well as glossy ibis are also frequently seen here. Ducks, including the blue-winged teal and common merganser, are most often seen in spring and fall.

When looking for birds on the outer beach, remember that the beach itself is privately owned, and respect the rights of property owners. In June I saw black ducks in the sound and great black-backed gulls on the offshore beaches. I recall a visit with a friend some years ago in mid-May when we saw at least sixteen species, including Canada and snow geese, buffleheads, American goldeneye ducks, and mallards as well as shorebirds like sanderlings, black-bellied plovers, and sandpipers.

The area of the sanctuary between the outer beach and the salt marsh is an excellent place to look for land birds, especially during migration.

Scheduled to open in mid- to late 1995, the Milford Point Coastal Center will be built at the Smith-Hubbell Wildlife Sanctuary on the site of the former Milford Point Hotel. It will serve as an education and research center, the only center in Connecticut to be dedicated exclusively to the study of the flora, fauna, and habitats of Long Island Sound.

Where: From I-95, exit 34, turn east onto US 1. Go .2 mile to a light at Lansdale Avenue. Turn right on Lansdale and follow it to where it intersects with Milford Point Road. Turn right onto Milford Point Road. You will cross Naugatuck Avenue and pass tennis courts and Court Street. Stay on Milford Point Road to the junction of Seaview Avenue. Turn right and continue about .3 mile to the Smith-Hubbell Wildlife Sanctuary. There is a sign at the entrance. The road forks right into the parking area. Do not take the road on the left, which is a private road.

Hours: Open year-round from sunrise to sunset.

Admission: There is no charge.

Best time to visit: Any time of year is bound to be interesting at this sanctuary, but you will see the greatest number of species of birds during spring and fall migrations. Winter is a good time to see large numbers of ducks in the offshore waters.

Activities: Bird-watching, photography, nature study. Not allowed are picnicking, swimming, and sunbathing.

Concessions: None.

Pets: No pets are allowed in the sanctuary. In addition, no dogs, even on a leash, are allowed on the beach (which is private) during nesting season, from April 1 to September 1.

For more information:

Connecticut Audubon Society, 118 Oak Street, Hartford, CT 06106-1514; 203-527-8737.

3

Central Connecticut

The birds love an easy way,
and in the valleys of the rivers
they find a road already graded for them;
and they abound more in such places
throughout the season
than they do farther inland.

— John Burroughs
Birds and Poets

Central Connecticut is a land of contrasts, ranging from large urban centers (Hartford and New Haven) to tranquil areas of fields, woods, and marshes bordering the Connecticut River and its tributaries.

The Connecticut River is a branch of the Atlantic Flyway. Great numbers of land birds, possibly as many as 200 species, follow the river valley during migration periods. At such times, woods that border the river and marshy areas provide food and resting places. In September, bird-watchers come to the Connecticut River to view a spectacular flight of hundreds and sometimes even thousands of hawks riding the thermal currents of air above the floodplain of the river as they migrate south.

Man, too, has always used the river as an avenue of transportation, from the time when Native Americans navigated the river in canoes and dugouts. Unfortunately, abuse of the river valley and degradation of the river's pure water paralleled industrial development in Connecticut. It is only in recent years that the impending loss of a great natural resource has been recognized and an effort made to clean up the river. Symbolic of people's interest in the river is the support being given to the effort to restore the Atlantic salmon to the Connecticut River and its tributaries. Although the project cannot yet be declared a success, the return of some salmon to their ancestral spawning grounds is proof of a vast improvement in water quality.

As you explore the river country, you will find trails to hike, rivers to fish or canoe, good areas for birding, views that are some of the most memorable in Connecticut, and a park where you can see tracks left in the mud by dinosaurs that roamed the Connecticut River Valley 200 million years ago.

HILL-STEAD MUSEUM

Hill-Stead Museum's Colonial Revival–style house, surrounded by gardens, farmland, and walking trails, transports you back to an earlier century. Located in Farmington, a town with many other interesting historic homes, Hill-Stead was designed as a retirement home for industrialist Alfred Atmore Pope and his wife, Ada Brooks Pope. Their architect daughter, Theodate, collaborated in designing the country home that was to be a showcase for the family's collection of French Impressionist paintings as well as a working New England farm. Outside, the design called for a broad front lawn overlooking the valley below and, to the rear of the house, a rustic walking garden filled with woodland plants and a more formal sunken garden planted with perennials.

It is thought that the sunken garden was lost sometime in the early 1940s when it degenerated due to wartime labor shortages. When Hill-Stead was opened to the public as a museum in 1946, this important landscape feature was missing. In 1983, the Connecticut Valley Garden Club and the Garden Club of Hartford undertook the restoration of the sunken garden. Using an early 1900s design for the garden found in the archives of landscape architect Beatrix Farrand, the garden restorers completed their work in 1986, having reestablished seventy-five varieties of plants, primarily perennials. Visitors may obtain a garden plan and plant list for the sunken garden in the museum bookstore. Last summer when my friend Milly and I visited Hill-Stead, we found all the old favorites here, including summer phlox, delphinium, foxglove, and bellflower.

We also joined a guided tour of the house, which is furnished the way it was when the Pope family lived there. The impressive art collection contains many paintings and etchings by the American artist James A. M. Whistler, a friend of the Popes. Most memorable of all, however, is the luminous light captured by Claude Monet in his seasonal haystack paintings.

I returned to Hill-Stead on a lovely spring day in April when the sun felt warm for the first time after an unusually cold, snowy winter. The red buds on the maple trees were beginning to swell, and in the woods the first delicate green leaves of wildflowers and shrubs transformed the drab winter landscape with their promise of new life. In the sunken garden, the soft pink blooms of a star magnolia signaled the arrival of spring, and I found glory-of-the-snow and daffodils just coming into bloom. A summerhouse in the center of the garden provided a quiet place to rest and enjoy the flowers.

From the parking area, I continued walking along the road past the old pump house, an orchard, a pond, and the farm meadows. Here, I was only dimly aware of the distant sound of traffic. I appreciated this view of the open fields and pond all the more for having just escaped from the heavy traffic on State 4, where commercial development has destroyed much of the surrounding countryside.

A map of the grounds and trails is available at the bookshop. One of several access points to the trails is just behind the parking area. From there I climbed a hill and entered a forest of tall hemlocks, where the only sounds were the calls of chickadees. A circular route takes you from the woods through fields and meadows and the old orchard back to the road near the pond. Special programs offered by the museum include nature walks to observe birdlife and wildflowers. The Hill-Stead trails also connect with the Metacomet Trail, part of the Connecticut Blue Trail system. The Metacomet Trail follows the traprock range running from the Hanging Hills of Meriden to the Massachusetts line for about forty-five miles.

A visit to Hill-Stead offers an opportunity to combine viewing an impressive art collection, including originals by Claude Monet, Édouard Manet, and Edgar Degas, with touring a delightful garden and enjoying a pleasant nature walk or longer hike on the Metacomet Trail.

Where: The entrance is on Mountain Road off State 10 in Farmington.
Hours: The grounds are open from 7:00 A.M. to 5:00 P.M. year-round. The museum is open Tuesday through Sunday. Hours vary with the season. Call 203-677-4787 for a schedule. Hour-long guided house tours of the museum are offered every half hour. Closed on major holidays.
Admission: Although there is no charge for admission to the grounds, a fee is charged for the house tour.
Best time to visit: May through August are the best months to

see the gardens. Spring wildflowers are best in May. October is special for fall foliage walks.

Activities: Hiking, jogging, birding, cross-country skiing, painting, sketching, and museum tours. Picnicking and fishing are *not* allowed. A schedule of special programs includes a nature series and a Sunken Garden Poetry Festival in the summer.

Pets: Not allowed.

For more information:

Hill-Stead Museum, 35 Mountain Road, Farmington, CT 06032; 203-677-4787.

DINOSAUR STATE PARK

The largest dinosaur track site in North America is in the Connecticut River Valley in the town of Rocky Hill. The site is preserved in Dinosaur State Park, a registered natural landmark. Here 500 of the early Jurassic tracks are on display, sheltered by the Exhibit Center's 122-foot geodesic dome.

The discovery of the tracks came in 1966 when bulldozer operator Ed McCarthy uncovered some unusual rocks during excavation work for a new state building. Action was then taken by the governor to preserve the site and establish a state park. The first excavation exposed nearly 1,500 tracks on a large area of bedrock. These tracks were eventually reburied for preservation. A second excavation in 1967 uncovered 500 more tracks, and those tracks are on display in the Exhibit Center. The tracks are of the type that had been named "Eubrontes" by a Massachusetts geologist in 1845.

When you look at the tracks preserved in the layers of sandstone, you are gazing at a record of life in the Connecticut River Valley 200 million years ago, when large carnivorous reptiles searched for prey along the edges of a large lake. Alone or in small groups, they waded in the shallow water searching for fish

**Tiger swallowtails feed on the nectar from ironweed,
butterfly weed, zinnias, and thistles**

or small crocodilians. In the age of the dinosaurs, Connecticut
had a semitropical climate. Some of the tracks you see were probably made as the dinosaurs crossed mudflats to rest in the upland
forests of cycads, ginkgoes, tall stiff evergreens, and lush ferns.

The exact nature of the dinosaur that made the tracks that
you will see in Dinosaur State Park remains a mystery. The
tracks are three-toed impressions that vary in length from ten to
sixteen inches. From the size of the tracks and the four-foot pace,
it is known that the adult dinosaurs were about eight feet tall and
twenty feet long. The skeletal remains that are the best match for

DISCOVERY OF FOSSIL TRACKS AND BONES OF DINOSAURS
The Connecticut Valley has a long history of fossil-track discoveries, dating back to the beginning of the nineteenth century. Edward B. Hitchcock, who for many years was the president and professor of natural theology and geology at Amherst College, became interested in the tracks in 1835. From that date on, until his death in 1864, much of his time was devoted to the discovery and study of fossil tracks. His collection of tracks became so large that a museum was built in Amherst to house it. However, Hitchcock never knew that he had discovered dinosaur tracks. As long as he lived, he believed that he was looking at the tracks of ancient birds. Nevertheless, his work and collection were invaluable to future dinosaur hunters like Othniel Charles Marsh and Richard Swann Lull, who in 1922 became director of Yale University's Peabody Museum of Natural History.

Although many tracks have been discovered, few fossil bones have turned up in the Connecticut Valley. The best skeleton found in Connecticut was discovered in a stone quarry near Manchester. It was a nearly complete skeleton, six or seven feet in length, and was named by Marsh "Anchisaurus colurus." The discovery of another species of dinosaur in the same quarry came too late. Only the back part of the skeleton was present. The front part had already been built into the abutments of a bridge!

the Eubrontes tracks are those of Dilophosaurus, a carnivorous dinosaur found in rocks of the same age in Arizona. A full-sized reconstruction of Dilophosaurus is on display in the Exhibit Center.

During the summer of 1994, the Exhibit Center was closed for improvements and renovations, including new lighting for better viewing, air-conditioning, and new permanent exhibits. In addition, the trackway boardwalk is being rebuilt to allow better access for visitors with disabilities. (Work should be completed by the spring of 1995.)

Outside the Exhibit Center is a track-casting area where

you may make a plaster cast of a real dinosaur track. Choose a good day for this project, because poor weather conditions will make casting difficult. You will need to bring a quarter cup of cooking oil, a five-gallon plastic bucket, ten pounds of plaster of paris, cloth rags, and paper towels. The entire process takes about thirty to forty-five minutes. Printed instructions are available at the park.

While dinosaur tracks are the big attraction, they are by no means the only reason to visit Dinosaur State Park. The discovery of the tracks led to the preservation of seventy acres of land in an otherwise heavily developed area south of Hartford. Three nature trails have been created, and a fourth is being planned. Depending on the season, you can see spring wildflowers, some of the many birds that are attracted to the area, swamp-dwelling creatures such as frogs and salamanders, and insects. Most interesting is the boardwalk trail through the heart of a swamp. The boardwalk was constructed by the Youth Conservation Corps during the summer of 1976. Walking this trail while listening to the calls of frogs from the depths of the swamp, surrounded by tall shrubs and trees, one finds it easy to slip back in time to the period when the great dinosaurs roamed this very area. A trail map and a checklist of birds seen at the park and in the vicinity are available at the trailhouse office. The list includes songbirds—such as thrushes, warblers, Baltimore and orchard orioles, and the scarlet tanager—as well as herons, the great horned owl, and the American woodcock. In all, 107 species have been recorded as seen within the boundaries of Dinosaur State Park.

The Meadow Nature Trail takes you past five small gardens, each of which has a different theme. The first is planted with garden flowers that are native to North America. In the past these perennials were overlooked by growers in favor of species from Europe and Asia. Recently the plant trade has begun to feature Connecticut's equally attractive native species, which are better suited to the hot, windy summers and cold winters. In another area, park staff are attempting to remove the most invasive species of European weeds, which settlers and their livestock brought with them from Europe and the Near East. It is widely feared that Connecticut's native wildflowers are being displaced by these hardy and aggressive plants. Two other gardens feature native meadow flowers, adapted to life in the sun, and meadow grasses. Contrary to popular belief, Connecticut was not entirely forested when the first settlers arrived from Europe. There were meadows in which native flowers and grasses flourished, supporting a great variety of insects, birds, and mammals.

Probably the favorite garden at the park is the Butterfly Garden, designed to attract butterflies for the enjoyment of visitors. Butterfly caterpillars need food plants such as the tall grasses, thistles, and milkweeds in the surrounding wildflower meadow. The adult butterflies need nectar plants like the flowers in the garden. It is hoped that these gardens will serve as a model and inspire homeowners to help these colorful insects survive. Butterflies are suffering a severe decline in Connecticut as land development destroys their natural habitat. As the display gardens' information sheet points out, "It would be a tragedy for us and our children to live in a world without butterflies."

Dinosaur State Park is open all year. In the winter, after a snowstorm, cross-country skiers follow the nature trails to look for animal tracks. Although many mammals are seldom seen, you can learn much from their tracks, which not only identify the animal but often tell you what that animal was doing. Common animal tracks you might see in the park are those of white-tailed deer, cottontail rabbits, opossums, gray squirrels, and deer mice. Kids may be interested in making castings of the animal tracks they discover. An information sheet available at the park identifies the common tracks and gives instructions for making a plaster-of-paris cast.

Visitors come to Dinosaur State Park to learn about the past history of our planet, but the park also teaches us about life today, demonstrating ways we can help protect our wildlife and native plants so that the rich diversity of life we now enjoy will still be here for our children and future generations.

Where: The park is on West Street, one mile east of I-91 (exit 23) in Rocky Hill.

Hours: Open daily 9:00 A.M. to 4:30 P.M. The track-casting area is open daily 9:00 A.M. to 3:30 P.M. May 1 to October 31. The Exhibit Center is open Tuesday through Sunday, 9:00 A.M. to 4:30 P.M. year-round, except for New Year's Day, Thanksgiving, and Christmas. The renovated Exhibit Center is expected to reopen in spring 1995. Call the park office for up-to-date information.

Admission: No fee is charged for admission to the park, but a fee is charged for admission to the Exhibit Center.

Best time to visit: The Exhibit Center may be crowded on summer weekends. Any other time is most enjoyable to visit this park.

Activities: Exhibit Center with fossil tracks and full-size reconstruction of a dinosaur. Walking on nature trails, viewing display gardens, making plaster casts of dinosaur tracks, picnicking, cross-country skiing, and searching for animal tracks. (No food or bicycles are allowed on the trails.) Programs and trail walks are offered by park naturalists.

Concessions: None.

Pets: Pets are not allowed on trails or in Exhibit Center.

For more information:

Dinosaur State Park, 400 West Street, Rocky Hill, CT 06067-3506; Infoline, 203-529-8423; staff, 203-529-5816.

WADSWORTH FALLS STATE PARK

Wadsworth Falls State Park is best remembered for its pleasant wooded hiking trails and thundering twenty-foot-high waterfall, which drops into a sunlit pool in the Coginchaug River. It is an easily accessible park with the entrance located in Middlefield on State 157. The park was given to the state in 1942 through the will of Colonel Clarence Wadsworth, a Middletown resident, who had devoted his life to civic endeavors and land preservation.

The wooded picnic area has tables and grills. Some tables overlook a small pond with a sandy beach, where you can swim in summer. Other facilities include rest rooms, changing rooms, and an outside water faucet.

The best time to hike the Main Trail to the falls is in the spring. Not only are the falls most impressive at this season, but also the mountain laurel is displaying its delicate pink blossoms. The trail begins just behind the picnic area and is marked with orange blazes. You cross a bridge over a small stream and, when the trail forks, follow the one to the right. Hiking through woods composed of maple, poplar, and birch, you pass a rare giant mountain laurel. Continuing along the trail, you notice the landscape changing, with more hickory, oak, and hemlock trees. The chattering of red squirrels is likely to be heard, and, depending on the time of day, you may catch a glimpse of a white-tailed deer. Hiking this trail one summer with a friend, I remember especially the feathery hemlocks along the slopes of the ravine. About three-quarters of a mile along, you reach a side trail to Little Falls on Wadsworth Brook. Big Falls is reached after a hike of a little more than one and a quarter miles from the start of the trail. Here the falling water cascades over volcanic trap-rock. The pool at the base of the falls is a favorite spot for trout fishermen.

Other short park trails that invite exploration are White Birch Trail, Deer Trail, Cedar Loop Trail, and Laurel Brook Trail.

Autumn, when the woods glow with the brilliant red leaves of the maples and the golden foliage of the hickories and birches, is also a good time to visit this park. I went there on a Sunday in late October and found myself in the company of many families who had come to hike or have a picnic amid the vibrant foliage on what turned out to be the last day of Indian-summer weather.

In winter, the parking area remains open for those who come to cross-country ski or snowshoe on designated trails. The Main Trail to the falls, Bridge Trail, White Birch Trail, and Cedar Loop Trail are all suitable for winter use.

Rangers are on duty during the summer season from Memorial Day through Labor Day but are not regularly available during the rest of the year. You can consult a carved map of the park's trails placed near the park entrance, and a trail map is also posted near the start of the Main Trail to the falls. However, if you are planning to hike here off-season, you may wish to obtain beforehand a trail map from the State Parks Division of the Connecticut Department of Environmental Protection.

Where: The park entrance is in Middlefield, on State 157, 1.6 miles southwest of the junction of State 66 and 157 in Middletown.

Hours: Open for day use from 8:00 A.M. to sunset daily as conditions permit.

Admission: A per-vehicle parking fee is in effect from Memorial Day through Labor Day weekend.

Best time to visit: The park is busiest during the summer months. Best time to hike is in the spring and fall. In winter, after a fresh fall of snow, it is also a good place for an outing on cross-country skis or snowshoes.

Activities: Hiking, fishing, swimming, picnicking, and cross-country skiing. No ranger-led activities are offered.

Concessions: None.

Pets: Not allowed on the beach or in the brook area. Dogs on a leash are permitted on the hiking trails.

For more information:

Bureau of Parks and Forests, Connecticut Department of

Environmental Protection, 79 Elm Street, P.O. Box 5066, Hartford, CT 06106-5066; 203-566-2305.

SALMON RIVER FOREST AND DAY POND STATE PARK

Five miles west of Colchester in eastern Connecticut, more than 6,000 acres of forested land have been preserved in Salmon River State Forest and adjacent Day Pond State Park. The acquisition of land for the state forest began in 1934 with the purchase of 286 acres on both sides of the Salmon River. Additional purchases have assured the preservation of this unspoiled natural area of the Salmon River Valley. A favorite haunt of trout fishermen and whitewater-canoeing enthusiasts, the river flows swiftly, swirling around boulders. Stands of hemlock line the riverbank, where the silence is broken by the murmuring of flowing water.

I first saw the Salmon River from the Comstock Covered Bridge, located just off State 16 in East Hampton. The Comstock Bridge, one of the few covered bridges left in Connecticut, was donated to the state by the towns of East Hampton and Colchester and restored by the Civilian Conservation Corps in 1936. The roadside area by the bridge has picnic tables. It's a prime spot to stop for a picnic or to fish, and you can walk across the bridge, which is limited to foot travel and connects the two parts of the forest.

The entrance to Salmon River State Forest is on the right, off State 16, just east of the covered bridge. On this warm day in late May, the area, which has a recreation field and picnic site, was uncrowded. White dogwoods were in bloom, and the sweet fragrance of pine filled the air as I walked toward the river through a stand of tall white pines. Along the riverbank are picnic tables and easy access points for fishing. I envied two girls who had placed their lounge chairs in the river, a delightful way to get some sun and keep cool at the same time.

The Salmon River, which is formed in Hebron by the con-
fluence of several brooks, flows in a southwesterly direction to
the Connecticut River at Haddam Neck. As a tributary of the
Connecticut River, the Salmon is playing an important role in the
effort to restore Atlantic salmon to the Connecticut River system.
Each spring, all along the Connecticut River from its source near
the Canadian border to where it empties into the sea near Old
Lyme, Connecticut, millions of fry and young salmon, seven to
nine inches long, are released into the river and its tributaries. At
Salmon River State Forest, two cement stream-fed "imprint"
ponds hold young salmon from hatcheries each spring before
they are released to depart on their long journey to the ocean.
After two years, the salmon find their way back as adults by
recognizing the odor of the water in which they were held. To
provide maximum protection for the young Atlantic salmon,
which are generally under nine inches in length, trout taken from
the Salmon River must be at least nine inches long, and any
salmon caught must be released immediately.

The effort to restore the salmon to their ancestral home has
its disappointments. It doesn't take much effort to imagine the
hazards the salmon encounter on a journey that takes them to
their feeding grounds off the coast of Greenland and back to New
England; but salmon are returning, and for those who have seen
one, it is a thrilling experience. The very fact that salmon can
now live in the Connecticut River is a great accomplishment in
itself. As recently as the mid-1950s, much of the river was still
badly polluted. For many, the return of the salmon is a symbol of
hope that we can reverse the damage that has been done to our
fragile planet. Perhaps most encouraging is the fact that the first
known truly wild salmon hatched at the mouth of the Salmon
River in the spring of 1992, but these native salmon are not due
to return to their river of origin until 1996.

The entrance to Day Pond State Park is off State 149, which
crosses State 16 a short distance east of the state-forest entrance.
The pond, which now attracts visitors with its sandy beach, was

constructed by a pioneering family by the name of Day. The pond water was used to turn a large waterwheel that powered the family's sawmill. Surrounding the park are inviting woodlands where oak, maple, beech, tulip, silver birch, hickory, and hemlock trees predominate. Picnic sites with tables and grills are scattered around the pond. A large picnic shelter, accessible to the handicapped, is located near the entrance overlooking the pond. It is equipped with tables and benches and two large fieldstone fireplaces for cookouts.

Spring is a good time to visit this park. On a day in late May, the woods were bright with the white blossoms of dogwood and the delicate pink blooms of wild azaleas. June, when the mountain laurel flowers, should be an equally good time. Wildflowers and ferns also abound. While I ate lunch at a site overlooking the pond, from somewhere hidden in the woods came the sound of classical music, a fitting accompaniment to the songs of birds, the whisper of a breeze through the trees, and the laughter of children down on the beach.

For hiking, access to a trail that loops four miles through the park and Salmon River State Forest is on the right, past the beach, just before the dam. This blue-blazed trail through mainly deciduous woods takes you to the crest of a hill from which you can view the Salmon River Valley.

Where: The covered bridge is on Comstock Bridge Road, off State 16 in East Hampton. The entrance to Salmon River State Forest is on the opposite side of State 16, just east of the bridge. Day Pond State Park is 5.5 miles west of Colchester off State 149.

Hours: Salmon River State Forest and Day Pond State Park are open from 8:00 A.M. to sunset year-round as conditions permit.

Admission: No charge at Salmon River State Forest. At Day Pond State Park there is a charge for parking on weekends and holidays; there is no charge off-season.

Best time to visit: Spring to see flowering shrubs, wildflowers, and ferns. Fall for hiking amid glowing foliage. It is best to visit before the start of hunting season, because hunting is allowed in Salmon River State Forest. Summer for swimming and picnics in Day Pond State Park. Winter for cross-country skiing in Salmon River State Forest.

Activities:

Salmon River State Forest—hiking, picnicking, fishing, hunting, and cross-country skiing.

Day Pond State Park—swimming, hiking, nature trail, picnicking, and fishing. (The pond is stocked with trout.) Picnicking and fishing are accessible to the handicapped.

Concessions: None.

Pets: No pets are allowed on the beach in Day Pond State Park. Pets on a leash are allowed on hiking trails.

For more information:

Bureau of Parks and Forests, Connecticut Department of Environmental Protection, 79 Elm Street, P.O. Box 5066, Hartford, CT 06106; 203-566-2305.

DEVIL'S HOPYARD STATE PARK

Devil's Hopyard State Park in East Haddam, where the Eight Mile River flows through a wild and scenic ravine, became Connecticut's twenty-first state park in 1919. Steep hillsides forested with hemlocks line the river and attract both migrant and nesting warblers, vireos, and thrushes. However, most of the 100,000 visitors who come to the park each year want to see the park's principal feature, Chapman Falls, which drop more than sixty feet over a series of steps in a Scotland schist stone formation. The falls were named after John Chapman, who once operated the grist- and sawmills at this location, known as "Beebe's Mills" after the original owner. The gristmill closed in 1854, but the sawmill continued in operation until the mid 1890s.

On a warm summer weekday I found the park uncrowded.

In fact, my friend Carolyn and I had one of the spacious, cool picnic sites along the river all to ourselves. After our lunch, we followed the trail to the top of Chapman Falls, where we looked down on the water cascading in a series of falls over ledges into quiet pools scoured out in the rock bed of the river. Along the sides of the gorge are large potholes, some of the finest examples of pothole stone formation in New England. Potholes are formed when a stone from upstream becomes trapped in an eddy and is spun around and around until it wears a cylindrical depression in the rock.

To superstitious early settlers, the potholes were a great mystery. Their attempt to explain how the potholes came to be there is the source of one of the many stories of how the park got its name. According to this legend, the Devil, passing by the falls, happened to get his tail wet, which made him hopping mad, mad enough to burn holes in the stone with his hooves as he bounded away!

Cross a covered bridge in the picnic area, and you are at the start of the Devil's Oven Trail, which climbs 150 feet over a series of ledges to a scenic overlook. Other trails lead to a trapper's sod hut, Baby Falls, and the Devil's Tombstone.

During May and June, Devil's Hopyard State Park is one of the best areas in Connecticut to see migrant and nesting birds. Near the beginning of the path that leads to the picnic area, you will notice some magnificent white oaks, which are favorite nesting sites for blue-gray gnatcatchers. You can easily identify this tiny blue-gray bird with its white belly, long, twitching tail, and wheezy but melodious warble. Its nest, fashioned of plant down and fibers held together with spiderwebs, holds four or five bluish eggs spotted with reddish brown. Other birds to look for in this area are redstarts, ovenbirds, and chestnut-sided, blue-winged, and black-and-white warblers.

In the thickets of mountain laurel that grow on the hillsides, you may catch a glimpse of the hooded warbler. The black hood

Everyone loves frogs, especially hungry kingfishers

and yellow face make the male easy to identify. In the hemlocks along the river near the picnic area, you may see the Acadian flycatcher, a rare species in Connecticut, which nests in this park. This shy bird of the deep forests is recognized by its greenish gray back, buff-colored wing bars, light eye rings, and sides washed with yellow.

Scarlet tanagers, rose-breasted grosbeaks, wood pewees, wood thrushes, veeries, and eastern bluebirds also nest in this park. Great-horned, barred, and screech owls nest in the area, as well as red-tailed and red-shouldered hawks. In early May, the river valley is on the flyway for migrating warblers, while in late August large flocks of nighthawks may be observed following this same route. For the migrating nighthawks, it is a long journey from Connecticut to South America, where they spend the winter.

If you camp in this park and get up very early in the morning, you'll have the best chance of seeing birds. Devil's Hopyard State Park has twenty-one wooded sites located near Chapman Falls. For those who like old-fashioned camping, it's a good place to come to enjoy bird-watching, hiking, or fishing. Each site has a table and a fireplace. The well and hand pump bring back memories of an earlier time. The sanitary facilities are of the primitive kind, too. In case of inclement weather, there is a shelter in the picnic area. This park is best for short-term camping in spring or fall. In summer the park may be crowded, and the no-swimming regulation leaves campers without any way to cool off on a hot day.

The Eight Mile River provides good fishing for brook trout. In addition, American and lamprey eels travel to the pool at the bottom of the falls each spring.

Where: Three miles north of the intersection of State 82 and 156.

Hours: Open for day use from 8:00 A.M. to sunset daily. The campground is open from mid-April to September 30. However, check with the State Parks Division office if you plan to camp before Memorial Day weekend or after Labor Day.

Admission: No fee for day use. There is a daily campsite fee for camping.

Best time to visit: Spring and fall when the park is uncrowded are the best times to visit.
Activities: Bird-watching, hiking, camping, stream fishing, and picnicking. No ranger-led activities are offered.
Concessions: None.
Pets: Not allowed in the campground or near the river or falls. Pets on a leash are allowed on wooded hiking trails.
For more information:
    Devil's Hopyard State Park, 366 Hopyard Road, East Haddam, CT 06423; 203-873-8566.

GILLETTE CASTLE STATE PARK

Gillette Castle State Park in Hadlyme is outstanding not only for its medieval-style fortress, the former home of the celebrated actor and playwright William Gillette, but also for the magnificent view it affords of the Connecticut River. Although the river has suffered three centuries of abuse by man, including pollution of its waters and uncontrolled development along its banks, the Lower Connecticut River Valley between East Haddam and Old Saybrook remains remarkably unspoiled. A sandbar at the mouth of the river has kept out deep-draft vessels and saved the river from the intensive development common to other major rivers. In recent years, federal, state, and local governments have spent more than $600 million in an attempt to clean up the Connecticut River and preserve its natural resources, including fish and wildlife. From Hartford south, the Connecticut becomes a tidal river.
    Downstream from Gillette Castle, near the mouth of the river in Old Lyme, ospreys nest on Great Island. The island has tidal channels that from November to April are frequented by many species of ducks, including buffleheads, greater scaup, and American goldeneyes. In addition, the Lower Connecticut River

Valley is the winter home of some twenty bald eagles. David and Deborah Ritchie report in their guide, *Connecticut Off the Beaten Path*, that in late winter or early spring, it is sometimes possible to stand on the main terrace of Gillette Castle and watch eagles soar over the river.

William Gillette and His Castle

Born July 24, 1853, William Gillette, noted actor and playwright, is best known for his portrayal of Sherlock Holmes. A Connecticut native, born and educated in Hartford, Gillette, at the height of his career in 1913, decided to build the home he had been dreaming of for years. Gillette was a man who loved nature in all its forms. He especially loved the Connecticut River and spent much of his free time cruising the river on his househoat, the *Aunt Polly*. He had almost decided to build his home near Greenport, Long Island, when, by chance, he anchored his boat near the east-bank slip of the Chester-Hadlyme ferry. Impressed by the rugged hill towering above the river, he decided to climb it the next morning. He was in the area of a series of hills along the river known as the Seven Sisters. When he reached the summit of the southernmost hill, he was so impressed by the splendid view of the river far below, bordered by forested hills and ridges of rock, that he immediately set about purchasing 122 acres of land adjacent to the ferry landing.

Gillette built his home on the summit of this hill and named it Seventh Sister. Constructed of native granite with southern white oak used in the interior, the castle took five years to complete and required the services of twenty-two skilled masons. With great inventive ability and a total disregard for conventional ways, Gillette designed everything for the interior as well as for the grounds of his home. Of the forty-seven doors within the castle, no two are exactly the same, and each has a handsome, intricately carved wooden latch. His creative ability is also evident in the built-in couches, a movable table on tracks, and the light switches of carved wood.

Gillette lived to be nearly eighty-four years old. Following his death in 1937, his estate was acquired by the State Park and Forest Commission. It had been William Gillette's wish that Seventh Sister and its extensive grounds be preserved for the benefit of others who would appreciate its great natural beauty as well as the creative genius that inspired the building of the castle. Today, the uniqueness of the castle draws over 100,000 visitors to tour it annually, hike the trails, and take in the sweeping views that were once a cherished part of William Gillette's life.

Chester-Hadlyme Ferry

Despite the popularity of Gillette State Park, it is still quite possible to find times to visit when the park is uncrowded. I found such a time on a weekday in late September when the first hint of autumn was just beginning to give color to the Connecticut hills. I stood on the main terrace for a long time enjoying the breathtaking view and the splendor of the terrace garden, still in bloom. Herring gulls circled over the river, and I watched a hawk riding the thermal currents. Far below, the ferryboat *Seldon III* was making its way back and forth across the Connecticut River. The Chester-Hadlyme Ferry has been in continuous operation since 1769. It is one of two historic ferries owned and operated by the Connecticut Department of Transportation. (The other is the Glastonbury–Rocky Hill Ferry, which, in operation since 1655, is the oldest continuously operating ferry in the United States.) The *Seldon III*, which departs from the ferry landing on State 148 in Chester from April 1 to the end of

November, can carry eight cars. Taking the ferry is a nice way to approach Gillette Castle.

Hiking Trails

Some of the trails in the park follow Gillette's own walking paths, which he constructed with steps and stone-arch bridges. Gillette, who was a railroad buff, also built on his property a three-mile-long narrow-gauge railroad. Portions of the railroad bed are today a hiking trail that winds its way through the woods and a rocky glen. Trail maps are available at the castle.

I followed one of the trails around a small lily-covered pond. The only sound was that of frogs diving beneath the lily pads as I approached. Near the water's edge, I watched a monarch butterfly sipping nectar in a clump of goldenrod.

Picnic Areas

Gillette Castle State Park is a fine place to go for a picnic. The main picnic area is wooded with oaks and hemlocks, which provide shade on a hot summer's day. However, on this cool fall day, I sought out a sunny table. While I ate lunch, I watched several gray squirrels feeding on the abundant crop of acorns. Nearer the castle, tables on a covered pavilion, as well as other choice picnic sites, offer a sweeping view of the river valley.

Canoeing and River Cruises

The Lower Connecticut River is a favorite area for boating, especially sailing and canoeing. There is a canoe-launching area within Gillette Castle State Park, and during the summer season

The characteristic "o-ka-LEEEE" of the red-winged blackbird
signals a marsh nearby

canoe rentals are available. For those who choose to explore the river by canoe, several state parks along the river provide shore access for picnicking, hiking, or camping. Selden Neck State Park, one and a half miles downstream on the left bank, covers 528 acres and is an undeveloped park with riverside campsites available from May 1 through September 30. Accessible only by water, the park has hiking trails with drinking water, fireplaces, and sanitary facilities for campers.

North of Gillette Castle State Park, about six miles south of Middletown on the east bank, Hurd State Park has good facilities for canoe camping, including water, tables, and a shelter. Two and a half miles below Hurd State Park, Haddam Island and Haddam Meadows State Park on the west bank are good places for boaters to stop for a picnic, but neither has camping facilities.

Although in its lower reaches the Connecticut River has retained much of its natural beauty, it is by no means free of development. In Haddam Neck, the Connecticut Yankee Atomic Power Company's nuclear generating station rises from the east bank. Also, the river has commercial traffic. If you decide to canoe the Connecticut River, you will have to watch out for tankers that make the journey from Hartford to Long Island Sound. Large yachts also travel the river, and their wakes can easily swamp a canoe or other small boat.

For those who prefer to let someone else do the navigating on this big river, Camelot Cruises offers a marvelous all-day cruise from Marine Park in Haddam, Connecticut, to Sag Harbor on Long Island. You will learn about the river's history along the way. The cruise ship departs every day, except Mondays, at 9:00 A.M. from June 27 through Labor Day. Fall foliage lunch cruises are also offered from September 21 through November 4.

Being on a boat in the river offers a great vantage point from which to observe birds. The whole Connecticut River Valley from the Connecticut Lakes in northern New Hampshire to Long Island Sound is a branch of the Atlantic Flyway. During

THE FUTURE OF THE LOWER CONNECTICUT RIVER

For nearly three decades, those who cherish the Connecticut River have been laboring to ensure its preservation for future generations. In 1966, then-Senator Abraham Ribicoff introduced legislation authorizing a comprehensive study of the river valley. The resulting report recommended that the federal government take action to preserve three of the most valuable sections of the river, including the Lower Connecticut River Valley. A subsequent bill drafted by Ribicoff and unanimously approved by the U.S. Senate created a Connecticut Historic Riverway in the area between East Haddam and Old Saybrook known as the "Gateway Area." However, the Historic Riverway National Park that Ribicoff envisioned never materialized. The proposal to create a national park along the river was defeated by residents in the towns bordering the river who feared loss of local control over land use. They also objected to additional land being set aside for public recreation.

Fortunately, the efforts to preserve the river didn't stop with the defeat of this bill. The Silvio Conte National Fish and Wildlife Act of 1991 authorized the U.S. Fish and Wildlife Service to consider the Connecticut River basin as a refuge. In the fall of 1993, the federal agency began informational hearings in the Lower Connecticut River Valley, explaining the proposal and gathering input from residents. The refuge proposal emphasizes cooperation with local groups as well as private owners. So far the proposal has received a generally favorable response. Residents who live near the river are quite aware of the abuse the river has suffered over the years and of the need for some kind of public control over land use. It is to be hoped that this Gateway area of the Connecticut River, site of Gillette Castle and winter home to bald eagles, an area that provides urgently needed feeding and resting areas for migrating birds, can enter the twenty-first century as part of the National Wildlife Refuge system.

---

spring and fall migrations, great numbers of land birds follow the river. In September, the Connecticut River is a good place to observe migrating hawks. While I saw only a lone hawk, hundreds and even thousands of hawks are sometimes seen during the peak days of the migration.

Fishing

In Colonial times, the Connecticut River had an abundant population of many species of fish. Salmon, weighing up to thirty pounds, and thousands of barrels of shad were harvested from the river. The construction of dams, which blocked access to the best spawning grounds, along with pollution of the water, changed all that. The salmon disappeared, and the shad run was reduced to a tiny fraction of its original numbers. In recent years, efforts to bring back the salmon through the construction of fish ladders and protection of spawning grounds has benefited the shad as well as the salmon. In addition, efforts have been made to clean up the river through the construction of sewage treatment plants. Salmon are once again returning to their ancient spawning grounds, and shad are returning to the Connecticut River in record numbers. The shad run usually begins in late April and ends by the middle of June. Largemouth bass are found in most sections of the river. In addition, panfish such as yellow perch and bluegill are abundant. A fishing license is required for resident as well as nonresident fishermen.

Although fish populations are increasing, further reduction of pollution is needed before a refreshing swim can be an enjoyable part of a visit to this historic river.

Where: Four miles south of East Haddam of State 82.
Hours: Open for day use from 8:00 A.M. to sunset daily. The castle is open for tours daily from Memorial Day through Columbus Day from 10:00 A.M. to 5:00 P.M. It is open weekends only, 10:00 A.M. to 4:00 P.M., after Columbus Day through the fourth weekend after Thanksgiving. It has become a

holiday tradition for many to visit the castle in December when the rooms are decorated for the holidays.

Admission: No fee for use of the park. An admission fee is charged to tour the castle.

Best time to visit: The park may be crowded during weekends in summer and especially during fall foliage season. Otherwise, any time is a good time to visit this park.

Activities: Hiking, picnicking, touring the castle, fishing, and canoeing.

Concessions: There is a gift and souvenir shop. From Memorial Day through Labor Day weekend, there is a food concession and rental canoes are available. For information on outfitting and transportation, contact North American Canoe Tours, Inc., 65 Black Point Road, Niantic, CT 06357; 203-739-0791 (off-season, 813-695-4666).

Pets: Pets on a leash are allowed in the park. Pets are not permitted inside the castle.

Other: Connecticut River Cruises offers one-and-a-half-hour cruises daily from June 20 through Labor Day (weekends only in spring and fall) on a replica Mississippi riverboat with onboard narration describing the history of the Connecticut River Valley.

For more information:

Gillette Castle State Park, 67 River Road, Hadlyme, CT 06439; 203-526-2336.

Camelot Cruises, Inc., 1 Marine Park, Haddam, CT 06438; 203-345-8591.

Connecticut River Cruises, Inc., 6 Marine Park, Haddam, CT 06438; 203-345-8373.

HAMMONASSET BEACH STATE PARK

In a state where much of the shoreline is privately owned, Hammonasset State Park in Madison, with its two miles of sandy beach on Long Island Sound, is crowded and often noisy in summer; but in spring and fall, the beach, fields, extensive marshes bordering the Hammonasset River, cedar woods, and thicket hedges belong to the bird-watcher, beachcomber, kite-flier, and refugee from the city who, tired of urban living, come to walk a deserted beach where the only sounds are the lap of gentle waves along the shore and the cry of seagulls overhead, a place where they can escape the smog and breathe fresh salt air.

I must confess that until I revisited this state park in 1994, I didn't associate such a place with Connecticut. When I think about favorite unspoiled mainland beaches in New England, places like Reid State Park in Maine come to mind, but on a beautiful spring day in May, I discovered that Hammonasset was not the park I remembered. Much has been done to restore the natural beauty of this coastal park. Plantings of beach grass and native shrubs have helped to stabilize the dunes and prevent further erosion. From the first parking area, a path leads between the dunes out to West Beach. It is important to obey the regulations and stay off the dunes. Beach plants are fragile and easily destroyed. Plantings of pine trees in the area between the beach and the parking lot provide shade for picnic tables overlooking the dunes and ocean. There are paths and a boardwalk along the beach, but nature lovers and beachcombers will probably prefer walking on the hard sand at the edge of the tide, where the retreating waves leave behind their treasure of seashells and shining pebbles.

Even the camping area, which I remembered as a large field with sites crowded together, has been vastly improved with the planting of trees and shrubs and the reduction in the number of campsites from more than 900 to 558.

From West Beach, it is a short walk to the large enclosed pavilion where a food concession operates during the summer months. There's a large deck with picnic tables overlooking the beach and sound.

From West Beach, I drove past East Beach to the parking area for Meig's Point, one of the best areas to see shore and water birds as well as migrating land birds in Connecticut. From the parking area, you can follow a loop road that borders the edge of a vast tidal marsh on the Hammonasset River. At the far end of this loop, you will find the beginning of the nature trail to Willard's Island, actually a woodland surrounded by tidal marsh, which provides a haven for migrating forest songbirds. In spring and fall, sparrows, warblers, thrushes, mockingbirds, and wood-peckers use the island as a stop-off point.

However, on this day I was looking for shorebirds, and scanning the salt marsh from the loop road turned out to be an exciting adventure. Out in the marsh were five medium-sized birds, which at a distance looked black. Through field glasses, I could see their bronzy chestnut feathers and long decurved bills. With the help of a couple of other bird-watchers and Peterson's *Field Guide to the Birds*, it was agreed that this small flock had to be eastern glossy ibis, a sighting that was later confirmed by the Audubon Shop in Madison, which maintains a record of current bird sightings in the area. The breeding range of this bird extends around the world. It is found in Spain, Greece, China, and Australia; but in the United States, until recently, the glossy ibis was found primarily in the marshes of Lake Okeechobee and along the Gulf Coast in Florida. In his book *North with the Spring*, Edwin Way Teale describes watching flocks of glossy ibis returning at sunset to their roost among the low willows on King's Bar in Lake Okeechobee. Some birds do wander north, and sightings in Connecticut are not as rare as they once were, yet watching these southern birds feeding in a Connecticut marsh was the highlight of the day for me.

Several killdeer were feeding in the marsh as well as in a shallow pool of rainwater in the field opposite the marsh. The dark double breastband makes these birds easy to identify. This hardy bird is found in meadows and along the borders of pasture ponds as often as it is found near salt water. Beetles, grasshoppers, and other insects are the killdeer's favorite foods. Its nest, which consists of a shallow depression in the ground lined with grass, is found in barren, open areas such as plowed fields or gravel bars. When they are disturbed, a loud "kill-dee" is their cry of alarm.

Later, two snowy egrets were sighted. This handsome bird was previously killed in great numbers to provide feathers for the millinery trade. By the beginning of the twentieth century, it had become rare and in danger of disappearing entirely from its favorite haunts — shallow ponds and quiet saltwater lagoons. Thanks to the passage of laws to protect the species and efforts to protect its breeding colonies, the species recovered, and today thousands of snowy egrets grace the shallow waters of our marshes and ponds.

This was also the right time to see the osprey nesting on the platform that had been erected for them toward the northern end of the marsh. The food of the osprey consists entirely of fish. For successful fishing, the osprey needs clear water and fish that swim or feed near the surface. In salt water, the common prey are mullet, menhaden, and herring. Since the ban on the use of DDT, the osprey population has been increasing in Connecticut. The provision of platforms in suitable areas has increased the availability of nesting sites for the osprey, a bird that almost disappeared in Connecticut because of the unwarranted use of a dangerous pesticide.

I went down to the outer beach at Meig's Point to eat lunch, sheltered from the wind by a huge boulder. Climbing the trail up this rocky point of land brings you to a good vantage point to look for seabirds. Today there were only a few ducks, but Dr. Noble Proctor, a leading authority on Connecticut birds, reports that loons, ducks, flocks of double-crested cormorants in spring and fall, and red-necked grebes in February have been seen from this location.

While I ate, herring gulls circled overhead, hoping for a snack. Herring and great black-backed gulls are both present at Hammonasset Beach. The gulls have become the English sparrows of the seabird world, disliked for their aggressive behavior toward other seabirds. Today, they are as common in the parking lots of shopping malls as they are on ocean beaches; yet, with their plaintive cry and graceful flight, the gulls circling just above the waves have always symbolized for me the beauty of the New England coast. Once again, on that spring day at Meig's Point, I welcomed the presence of the gulls.

Sawteeth and a hooked bill enable mergansers to feed on slippery fish

Where: One mile south of exit 62 off I-95 in Madison.

Hours: Open for day use from 8:00 A.M. to sunset daily, year-round as conditions permit. Campground is open from the weekend before Memorial Day weekend until November 1. Check with the park office first if you are planning to camp before Memorial Day or after Labor Day weekend.

Admission: Daily parking fee during the summer months. In addition, there is a charge on weekends only from April 15 through Memorial Day and again from Labor Day through the end of September. Campers pay a nightly fee per campsite.

Best time to visit: Spring and fall to see waterfowl and land birds. The park is crowded in summer.

Activities: Swimming, scuba diving, camping, fishing, bird-watching, picnicking, hiking, and boating. During the summer season, a nature center is open, and there are interpretive programs. A newly constructed observation platform at Meig's Point opened in May 1994.

There is excellent fishing from the stone jetty constructed during the winter of 1978–79. You can fish for saltwater species such as flounder and bass. A launching site is provided for fishermen who bring their own boats.

The campground has 558 mostly open sites. Facilities include flush toilets, showers, and a dumping station. Individual fireplaces are not provided.

Concessions: A food concession is operated during the summer months.

Pets: Not allowed.

For more information:

Hammonasset Beach State Park, Box 271, Madison, CT 06443; campground office, 203-245-1817; park office, 203-245-2785.

The Audubon Shop, 871 Boston Post Road, Madison, CT 06443. Call 203-245-9056 for information on birds seen and spring bird walks at Hammonasset Beach State Park.

4

Northeastern Connecticut

*. . . for those who find their pleasure
out-of-doors, . . . all the years of existence
represent a long love affair with the earth. . . ."*

— Edwin Way Teale
A Naturalist Buys an Old Farm

Connecticut's "Quiet Corner" is sparsely populated, character-
ized by dense forests of white pine and northern hardwoods and
many lakes and ponds, a rolling plateau of land divided by three
rivers—the Natchaug, the Willimantic, and the Quinebaug. State
forests and parks have helped to preserve much of the region's
forestland along with some of the most scenic lakes and ponds.
My favorite park in this area is Bigelow Hollow State Park,
where the lakes and forests remind me of those in Maine and
Ontario.

It is this region of Connecticut that author and naturalist
Edwin Way Teale and his wife, Nellie, chose for their retirement

home. Today you can visit their farm, Trail Wood, now a sanctuary of the Connecticut Audubon Society.

"For those who find their pleasure out-of-doors," Connecticut's northeast corner will provide a lifetime of memories of quiet walks and scenic places, where the possibility of seeing wildlife turns even an afternoon stroll into an exciting adventure.

BIGELOW HOLLOW STATE PARK

One of my favorite places in northeastern Connecticut is a state park that reminds me of the lakes and forests of Maine and Ontario. There is a reason for this feeling of being in the north country, for Bigelow Hollow State Park in Union is an example of a Canadian Zone pocket of forest that attracts some species of birds that usually nest far to the north. Magnolia, Nashville, black-throated blue, and blackburnian warblers nest in the spruce and pine woods. In the thick growth of mountain laurel that covers the hillsides, the solitary vireo builds its nest. Here, too, on the rocky slopes, the winter wren, a bird more likely to be found breeding in northern Ontario, will nest, and its song, a succession of warbles and trills, may be heard on a spring bird walk.

If you want to see even more species of warblers, plan to visit this park in early May. In Connecticut, the height of the warbler migration occurs during the first two weeks of May, and the route of nearly all these wood warblers takes them through Bigelow Hollow State Park.

I first discovered this park several years ago in late May on a bird-watching trip to eastern Connecticut. The drive took me north on State 198 through the Natchaug River Valley, where lilacs were in bloom and a new growth of foliage and spring wildflowers brightened the woods and fields. When I turned north on State 171, I entered another world of sunlit evergreen forests. I began to see birds even before I reached the park. A bright flash of orange-and-black wings was a Baltimore oriole. A gray bird, the size of a robin, with large white patches on its wings and tail was also easy to recognize as an eastern mockingbird; and I had a good look at a pair of purple finches when I slowed down for two birds in the middle of the road!

At the junction with State 197, I continued west. A right turn, which is easily missed, takes you into the 513-acre park, which contains two lakes. Stopping first at the lower lake, known as Bigelow Pond, where there is a nice picnic area, I walked down to the water's edge and scanned the surface of the pond and marshy areas along the shore. While I failed to spot any activity, I knew that wood ducks and occasionally hooded mergansers nest in this area. Both have benefited from the nesting-box program. The pond and the upper lake (Mashapaug Lake) also attract other waterfowl, including mallards, black ducks, ring-necked ducks, and great blue and green herons. During migration periods, birders may even see common loons or pied-billed grebes.

Leaving the first parking area, I drove to the end of the park road, where there is a second parking area and a gravel boat-launching ramp on the shore of Mashapaug Lake. This upper lake is a jewel with clear water, deep blue in the center where it mirrors the sky, and shades of emerald green in the coves, where tall spruces and hemlocks grow to the water's edge. Inviting rocky ledges and small islands add to the feeling that you are far to the north. To the left of the boat ramp, a trail leads through the woods to a picnic area on a forested point overlooking the lake. Birds were everywhere, but difficult to see as they alighted in the very tops of tall trees. Listening to a medley of spring birdsong, I ate my lunch and watched a small flock of white-throated sparrows feeding nearby. The nest of this sparrow, made of grass and moss, is often found along the brushy edges of a spruce forest.

In it, the female lays four or five spotted greenish eggs. The clear, pensive notes of the white-throat's song are synonymous with the arrival of spring in the Northern forests.

According to Dr. Noble Proctor, an authority on Connecticut birds, both ruby-crowned and golden-crowned kinglets, birds that usually nest far to the north in the spruce forests of Canada, are known to have nested in Bigelow Hollow State Park. One of the smallest birds of the coniferous forests, the golden-crowned kinglet builds its nest from moss, lichens, and even spiderwebs. The inside is lined with feathers and fur, and the nest holds eight or nine cream-colored eggs speckled with brown. This park is one of only two places in Connecticut where both species of kinglets are known to have nested.

Other species that nest in the park include brown creepers, several species of hawks, and pileated woodpeckers. Great-horned, barred, and saw-whet owls also nest in this area.

From the picnic area, I continued along the trail, which follows the western shore of the lake and leads to another favorite spot with huge rock ledges, perfect for sunning or picnicking.

It was late afternoon when I stopped again at Biglow Pond. The wind had died down, and I watched a red canoe glide silently across the smooth surface of the pond. Three male redstarts were flying through the hemlocks in search of insects. I could understand why, in the West Indies, the Spaniards called these birds "candelitas," for the flashes of bright orange on their wings and tails seemed to light up the dark forest of evergreens. A flock of ducks flew across the pond as the sun dropped below the horizon and the shadows of evening spread across the water.

Winter, when the park's evergreen forests attract evening grosbeaks, pine siskins, and red crossbills, is also a good time for birding. Less frequently seen species include redpolls and pine grosbeaks. Saw-whet owls frequent the pines near Bigelow Pond.

Both of the lakes are popular with fishermen. The waters

are stocked with brown and rainbow trout. Boats are limited to 10 mph. The lack of speedboats and development along the shores make both lakes good for canoeing. Mashapaug Lake's hard sand and gravel bottom and clear water attract scuba divers and swimmers. Swimming, at your own risk, is allowed.

Nipmuck State Forest, which covers 8,058 acres, adjoins Bigelow Hollow State Park. The Nipmuck Trail passes through the park and state forest. Access is off State 171, a short distance from the park entrance.

Where: Two miles east of Union on State 197.

Hours: From 8:00 A.M. to sunset daily.

Admission: Fee for parking on weekends and holidays from Memorial Day through Labor Day weekend.

Best time to visit: Spring and fall to see birds. For other activities, any season is a good time to visit this park.

Activities: Bird-watching, picnicking, fishing, scuba diving, swimming (no lifeguard), canoeing, and hiking.

Concessions: None.

Pets: Not permitted near the lakes. Pets on a leash are allowed on the Nipmuck Trail.

For more information:

Bureau of Parks and Forests, Connecticut Department of Environmental Protection, 79 Elm Street, P.O. Box 5066, Hartford, CT 06106-5066; 203-566-2305.

TRAIL WOOD, THE EDWIN WAY TEALE MEMORIAL SANCTUARY

Located in Hampton, in the rolling country of northeastern Connecticut, is a special place known as Trail Wood, the Edwin Way Teale Memorial Sanctuary. For the last twenty years of his life, Trail Wood was the home of the naturalist, writer, and photographer Edwin Way Teale and his wife, Nellie. Winner of a Pulitzer prize for his four-volume *American Seasons* and the John Burroughs Medal for distinguished nature writing, Teale and his wife had traveled through all the forty-eight states, yet when it became possible for them to move to the country, it was an old farm outside the small village of Hampton that they chose. One look at the property, and they knew it was the place they had been searching for. If you visit Trail Wood, you will understand why.

The farmhouse, built in 1806 and surrounded by 156 acres of fields, woods, and wetlands, became their home for the next twenty years. These years spent exploring Trail Wood and their observations of its wildlife and plants during all seasons of the year became the subject of Teale's last two books, *A Naturalist Buys an Old Farm* (1974) and *A Walk Through the Year* (1978).

Shortly before Teale's death on October 18, 1980, Edwin and Nellie asked the Connecticut Audubon Society if it would help perpetuate Trail Wood as a wildlife sanctuary. Mrs. Teale retained life tenure of the farmhouse and its immediate environs and continued to live there until her death in 1993.

At present, the trails of the sanctuary are maintained by the Friends of Trail Wood, a local group dedicated to the literary and natural-history legacy of Edwin Way Teale. Their goal is to maintain the trails as they existed during Teale's lifetime and to perpetuate his quest for wildlife preservation and scientific study. All trails are open year-round to the public for nature walks and hiking. Guided hikes can be arranged. The excellent trail map, available from a box near the house, identifies all the points of interest with the names given them by the author and his wife. It is suggested that those planning to visit contact a member of the Friends of Trail Wood first. For the first-time visitor, a guided hike is recommended because there are many intersecting trails that can be confusing. The western boundary is 12,935-acre

Both parents team up to feed blue-heron chicks

Natchaug State Forest. Waterproof boots are advisable for the wet season for crossing brooks and wet areas.

From time to time, the Friends of Trail Wood schedule guided hikes, which include visiting the naturalist's writing cabin and home. I was able to join one of these "literary nature walks" in October 1993. It was a part of "Walking Weekend," a three-day event on Columbus Day weekend, which gave participants an opportunity to explore the rich historic, cultural, and natural features in the twenty-five towns that constitute the proposed Quinebaug–Shetucket Rivers National Heritage Corridor.

When I reached Trail Wood, the meadow parking area was nearly filled to capacity, and I was just in time to join the next walk. For those who treasure Teale's books, there was a sadness associated with seeing the empty house with its great fireplace where on winter evenings Edwin and Nellie liked to sit and read and "feel the warmth of the dancing flames and glowing coals." Some of Teale's marvelous photographs are on the wall of his office and library, where he did much of his writing. Since I was there, the Connecticut Audubon Society has found tenants who will reside at the farm and help look after the property.

In May 1963, four years after moving to Trail Wood, the Teales began the construction of a pond in a swampy area southwest of the house. The pond attracted all kinds of wildlife, and today it looks as if it had always been part of the landscape. As we followed the trail that Teale had created around the pond, I recalled his observations as he and Nellie watched life come to the pond that first summer. First there were aquatic insects— water striders and whirligig beetles. Then bullfrogs found a home in the pond, and the first water plants took root. In the evenings, swallows would swoop low over the water to drink.

In the ensuing years, the pond became home for other wildlife. Schools of minnows swam in the shallows, and bluegills and largemouthed bass could be observed from the rustic bridge across Stepping Stone Brook. The fish attracted kingfishers to the pond. In addition to the bullfrogs, five other species of frogs laid their eggs in the Trail Wood pond—the spring peeper, the gray tree frog, the green frog, the pickerel frog, and, on rare occasions, the leopard frog. "Turtle Rock" became the favorite sunning place of the painted turtles. The Teales were not the only ones who followed the trail around the pond. On one October morning, they saw a mink on the path, and on another day Nellie watched a long-tailed weasel hunting beside Driftwood Cove.

The author built a rustic screened-in summerhouse overlooking the pond. Here, on summer evenings, he and Nellie were fond of eating a picnic supper while observing the life around them. Once, after sunset, they watched a great blue heron wading in the shallow water near shore. Just below the summerhouse, they watched robins, catbirds, red-winged blackbirds, grackles, thrushes, and scarlet tanagers bathing in the shallow water. Soon after the pond was built, muskrats came to inhabit it. Watching their activities provided an endless source of fascination during those evenings spent in the summerhouse. Describing their experience, Teale wrote, "We watch these aquatic animals during warm twilights in summer, bringing home food, swimming back and forth across the pond, trailing long ripples, silver V's that grow more silver as the water becomes more dark and mirrorlike."

The pond trail also took us to Teale's writing cabin, a rustic log cabin furnished with a woodstove, oil lamp, desk, and shelves. Teale often came here to read and write, uninterrupted by ringing telephones. Although the cabin is only a five-minute walk from the house, he was surrounded by scenes that reminded him of northern Maine. The pond, only an acre in size, is surrounded by undisturbed woods and hillsides that provide a sanctuary for wildlife. My lasting impression of this walk on the pond trail was of the incredible variety of plants, animals, and birds sustained by this one small pond.

From the pond, we headed north, following the Old Woods

Road trail much of the way to the Beaver Pond. This was the Teales' favorite path and the one they most often trod. From the summerhouse, the trail leads north past Woodcock Pasture, where each year, usually in March after the snows melted, Edwin and Nellie would listen with growing anticipation at dusk each day for "the magical flight-song of the woodcock." The trail, which crosses Fern Brook, passes through an area that in summer is filled with cinnamon and interrupted ferns. The leaves of hickories, oaks, and maples made the woods bright with autumn color for our hike. I remember the dark green Christmas ferns carpeting the whole slope of the ridge. In all, twenty-six species of native ferns grow at Trail Wood, including grape, royal, and sensitive ferns; the silvery spleenwort; the evergreen wood fern; and the New York fern. In addition, several varieties of club mosses carpet the ground.

A trail that crosses Old Woods Road is known as Old Colonial Road. Wagons and carriages, and perhaps even stage-coaches, once rolled over this ancient path.

Finally we reached the Beaver Pond in the wildest and most northern part of the sanctuary. It was Nellie who, while walking Old Woods Road one early October afternoon, discovered that where a swamp had previously been there was now a pond covering about three acres. Beavers had blocked the flow of Hampton Brook where it passed through a gap in an old stone wall. Some thirty years later, this original dam, 125 feet long, built of mud and sticks, is still kept in good repair by the industrious inhabitants of the pond. I recalled Teale's description of a memorable night spent beside the pond watching beavers in the moonlight. When I visited the pond, the large old beaver lodge appeared to be abandoned, but a newer lodge toward the north end of the pond showed signs of activity from the freshly cut branches near the entrance. The Beaver Pond has also attracted other wildlife, including frogs, turtles, dragonflies, wood ducks, and Louisiana water thrushes, which Teale observed searching for food in the mud at the edge of the pond.

Following a trail along the edge of the Beaver Pond, we reached "Deerfield." Deer are frequently seen at Trail Wood, especially in this northern part of the sanctuary. One can often find their hoofprints in the moist ground or their trails through the woods. Deer had been seen that morning in a field near the house where, in the fall, they come to eat the fruit of the old apple trees. Teale wrote of finding saplings with the bark removed and the wood polished by bucks rubbing the velvet from their antlers. For Edwin and Nellie, the memory of seeing a magnificent antlered buck seemed "symbolic of all the beauty and wildness of [their] woods."

On the return hike, we followed Old Colonial Road, and near the top of the ridge, we stopped to examine the stub of a huge chestnut tree. The tree had died in the 1920s from the blight that swept through New England. Today most chestnut tree seedlings are killed by the blight before they can reach maturity, but there is ongoing research to develop a strain that will be resistant to the blight. We can only hope that someday this magnificent tree can once again grow in New England forests.

Spring is also a good time to visit Trail Wood. In 1974, when *A Naturalist Buys an Old Farm* was published, the bird count for species seen at Trail Wood stood at 144 species. Teale writes about awakening to a dawn chorus of voices that included wood thrushes, veeries, bluebirds, robins, purple finches, catbirds, scarlet tanagers, rose-breasted grosbeaks, and northern orioles. He estimated that between forty-five and fifty species of wild birds nested in the woods and fields near the house. In the first days of spring, they would often hear the bluebirds singing in the apple trees. "When we first hear that gentle sound," Teale wrote, "some of the hardness of winter softens within us."

Trail Wood can also be a good destination in winter, when a walk on cross-country skis or snowshoes may reveal animal tracks in the snow. When the Teales were living there, they provided a feeding area for both birds and wild animals. Especially toward the end of winter when food was scarce, the author and his wife would observe gray foxes, skunks, opossums, and raccoons at the feeding area just outside the kitchen door.

Edwin and Nellie Teale never felt as if they owned Trail Wood. They were simply sharing the land with all its other inhabitants. "We are one," Teale wrote, "with the robin among the wild cherries in the sunshine." For them, having the deed to the property conferred responsibility—the responsibility of guardianship—to protect the woods, the streams and fields, and all the wildlife that dwells there. Now that responsibility has passed to others, and other feet walk the familiar trails, perhaps discovering, as the author and his wife did, that "for those who find their pleasure out-of-doors, . . . all the years of existence represent a long love affair with the earth."

Where: From US 6, east of Clark's Corner, turn north on State 97 to Hampton, then west on Kenyon Road to Trail Wood.

Hours: All trails are open year-round to the public for unguided nature walks and trail hiking.

Admission: No admission charge. However, those who wish to help in the maintenance of the sanctuary may join the Friends of Trail Wood or contribute to the Edwin Way Teale Memorial Sanctuary Fund established by the Connecticut Audubon Society to help maintain Trail Wood and its wildlife communities.

Best time to visit: Any time of the year is a good time to visit. Edwin and Nellie Teale's years at Trail Wood were devoted to a study of nature's seasonal changes. It is hoped that visitors to Trail Wood through their explorations and observations may add to the knowledge about its living communities.

Activities: Nature walks and study, nature photography, hiking, cross-country skiing, and snowshoeing. Guided hikes are provided by the Friends of Trail Wood. Special programs and activities may be arranged by the Connecticut Audubon Society.

Concessions: None.

Pets: Not allowed.

Facilities: There is a toilet facility at the edge of the parking area. However, you need to bring your own supply of drinking water.

For more information:

Connecticut Audubon Society, 118 Oak Street, Hartford, CT 06106-1514; 203-527-8737.

To arrange a guided hike, contact a member of the Friends of Trail Wood: John Woodworth, 203-455-9650, or Wendell Davis, 203-455-9143.

GAY CITY STATE PARK

Located on the Hebron-Bolton town line, along State 85, Gay City State Park is best known for its historical significance as the site of one of Connecticut's early settlements. Gay City was first settled in 1796 by a religious sect led by Elijah Andrus. It was named for John Gay, who became village president in 1800. A sawmill was built on the Blackledge River, and later a woolen mill was constructed on a site one-fourth mile below the present pond. In 1830, the mill was destroyed by fire. A paper mill, built by Dr. Charles Sumner, kept the town alive until the Civil War. When it too caught fire and burned in 1879, it signaled the end of Gay City. Today, white-tailed deer roam what was once the main street of the village; and except for the small graveyard near the park entrance, a few cellar holes, and the remains of the woolen mill, there is little evidence that families once lived here. What man abandoned, nature has reclaimed.

A system of ten numbered trails connect with each other, making it possible to do a number of loop hikes. Trails connect with the Shenipsit Trail to the west, which runs through Meshomasic and Shenipsit State Forests to the border of Massachusetts. Possum and Partridge Trails are named for the park's wildlife. A trail map is available from the Office of State Parks and Recreation. If you hike in the morning or late afternoon in the spring or fall, there is always the possibility of seeing deer on these forest trails. However, they are wary because hunting is allowed in the adjacent state forests.

In early spring, you may flush a woodcock from a wetland area where there is good cover. A little larger than a quail, this chunky brown bird, with its barred crown and long bill, always looks to me as if it belongs at the edge of the tide on a sand beach. If you are at the park near dusk in late March or early April, you may be fortunate enough to hear the aerial mating song of the male. Only once in spring have I been able to observe this bird in its wild flight. Its magical song begins at the height of its ascent. Then it plunges back to earth, often landing in thick brush in the center of a swamp.

**Woodcocks blend in so perfectly with dead leaves
that they're very hard to see**

Gay City State Park is also a good place to look for woodland birds such as thrushes, warblers, vireos, chickadees, nuthatches, and woodpeckers. Also in spring, the woods may resound with the drumming of the male ruffed grouse. The throbbing sound may be repeated, slowly at first, and then with increasing speed until it abruptly stops. The grouse produces the sound by beating its wings. The male drums to call to its mate, to challenge another cock, or sometimes for no reason at all discernible to man. Whatever prompts this display, listening for this sound is for me part of the joy of a hike in Connecticut woods, along with listening for spring peepers, hearing the call of wild geese flying overhead, and catching a glimpse of a white-tailed deer.

The South Trail goes through a wetland area in the southwestern part of the park. After crossing a swampy area on a long boardwalk, the trail climbs gradually to an overlook from which you can look down on an active beaver pond. A nice sand beach makes the pond a good place to come in summer for swimming and a picnic. Facilities include tables with fireplaces, a rest-room building, and drinking water. The picnic area and rest rooms are accessible to the handicapped.

Gay City State Park is also one of my favorite places to go hiking in the fall. When the oaks and maples along the park road turn to brilliant shades of red and gold, my thoughts go back to that earlier time when this road was the main street of the village. Left off the park road is Gay City Road, once the main route between Gay City and Glastonbury and the Connecticut River, but now a hiking trail where you are likely to encounter small mammals such as chipmunks and gray squirrels as well as woodland birds.

In winter, you can strap on cross-country skis or snowshoes to explore Gay City State Park. The small parking area near the entrance is plowed, and since the park is located just off State 85, it is easily accessible in winter. Moreover, where a trail crosses a stream, the state has built good bridges that facilitate use of the trails in winter. Tracks you are likely to spot in the snow include deer, opossums, squirrels, rabbits, and ruffed grouse. In addition, on any woodland winter walk in Connecticut, there is now the possibility of discovering the tracks of wild turkeys. Since it is the largest of our wildfowl, with tracks five inches long, you can easily identify it. The three front toes and the tip of the hind toe off to one side register in the track. The turkeys travel in small flocks of six to twelve birds. At night they roost in trees, usually returning each night to the same roosting grounds in wooded bottomlands. Wild turkeys became extinct in Connecticut in 1813 as a result of the destruction of the forests and unregulated hunting. The State Conservation Department began efforts in 1975 to bring the wild turkey back to Connecticut. The effort was so successful that today it is estimated that there are more than 6,000 wild turkeys in the state feeding on a diet of acorns, berries, grass, and insects.

Some people may come to Gay City State Park to look for clues to its vanished past, but for me, its present wildlife and wooded trails and pond hold more interest, making it a favorite place to hike, swim, or cross-country ski.

Where: Three miles south of Bolton on State 85.

Hours: 8:00 A.M. to sunset daily, year-round, as conditions permit.

Admission: A parking fee is charged weekends and holidays during the summer season.

Best time to visit: Spring and fall for hiking and viewing wildlife, summer for swimming, winter for cross-country skiing.

Activities: Hiking, picnicking, swimming, fishing, cross-country skiing, ice skating, exploring a historic site. No ranger-led activities, but a ranger is on duty during the summer season. At this time, trail maps are available at the park.

Concessions: None.

Pets: Not allowed on the beach or in the pond. Pets on a leash are permitted on wooded hiking trails.

For more information:

Bureau of Parks and Forests, Connecticut Department of Environmental Protection, 79 Elm Street, P.O. Box 5066, Hartford, CT 06106; 203-566-2305.

THE MOOSUP RIVER

The Moosup River, which rises in Rhode Island, flows south and then west into Connecticut through the towns of Oneco, Almyville, Moosup, and Central Village, where it joins the Quinebaug River below Wauregan.

In very early spring when the water level is high, the central portion of the river from the Almyville Dam to the State 14 bridge below Central Village offers a 3.5-mile run with class I and class II rapids for experienced canoeists able to maneuver around rocks. In this stretch of the river, the free flow of the water has been blocked by several dams.

However, when I think of the Moosup River, I think of the upper reaches and a private family campground, River Bend Campground, in Oneco, where flocks of wild geese stop to feed and rest during spring and fall migrations. At George and Nancy Marchacos's campground you can pitch your tent in a fragrant grove of white pine trees surrounded by twenty-eight acres of woodlands and open fields. With your own or a rental canoe, you can put in at the campground pond and paddle upstream into Rhode Island. In its upper reaches, the Moosup, at least in summer, is mainly flat water with only a gentle current, which makes it possible to paddle in both directions. Above Oneco, there are no dams. Here the river meanders through isolated, wild, wooded country with extensive marshes that are a haven for many birds, animals, and plants. In Rhode Island, this stretch of

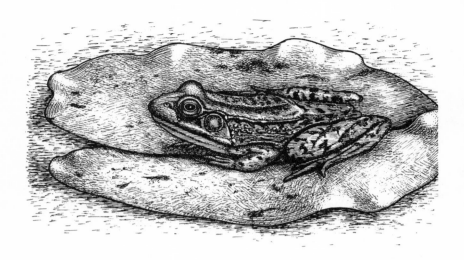

A green frog pauses on a lily pad

river is protected by state forestland in recognition of the river's value to wildlife and to man. On the Connecticut side, the Moosup State Park Trail follows the course of the river from Moosup to the Rhode Island state line.

If you canoe upstream, you will pass several cottages. Beyond this point, you paddle for seven miles through unspoiled country toward the river's headwaters. Stained dark brown by the natural tannins in it, the water reflects the clouds overhead and the trees lining the banks. You may find your way blocked by a fallen tree or a beaver dam. That is part of the adventure. As the canoe glides silently along, you may see ducks rising from the marshes or turtles sunning themselves on a partly submerged log. My favorite memory is of a great blue heron that spread its wings and took flight just a short distance ahead of the canoe.

If you stop to explore along the banks of the river, you may find the tracks of deer and raccoons, and gnawed evergreen branches or oval pellets may tell you where a porcupine has been. In addition, many wildflowers grow along the river, including the spectacular red cardinal flower and the wild pink orchid known as the moccasin flower.

The Moosup River is also a fisherman's paradise. It is stocked with trout by both Rhode Island and Connecticut. Fishing is good for trout, largemouth and smallmouth bass, and pickerel.

Where: From I-395, exit 88, drive 5.5 miles east on State 14A to Oneco. Turn right at the "River Bend" sign just before the bridge.
Hours: River Bend Campground is open from April 19 through October 7.
Admission: Overnight, weekly, and seasonal fees for camping. Tent and travel trailers, cabins, canoes, and pedal boats are also rented.
Best time to visit: Late spring or summer for canoeing and camping. Early mornings or weekdays are the best times for quiet canoe trips to see wildlife.
Activities: Canoeing, camping, fishing, wildlife watching, swimming (pool), and hiking. River Bend Campground also offers complete recreational facilities for families as well as a weekend recreation program.
Other facilities: Most campsites have water and electric hookups for RVs, and there are some sites with full hookups. There are also modern rest rooms with hot showers, laundry facilities, and a store.
Pets: Pets on a leash are allowed at the campground.
For more information:
River Bend Campground, Box 23, Route 14A, Oneco, CT 06373; 203-564-3440.

For information on the Moosup State Park Trail: Bureau of Parks and Forests, Connecticut Department of Environmental Protection, 79 Elm Street, P.O. Box 5066, Hartford, CT 06106-5066; 203-566-2305.

5

Southeastern Connecticut

We heard a great horned owl call, far away.
Darkness was coming down the hills.
In the pale water before me,
an otter curved momentarily,
and the silver wake of a beaver flashed,
far down the other lake.

— Florence Page Jaques
Canoe Country

Florence Page Jaques wrote about the vast lake country of northern Minnesota, Ontario, and Manitoba, where the absolute free-
dom of a canoe trip gives "every hour an intense lucidity." The
chain of rivers, lakes, and ponds in southeastern Connecticut,
many of which are protected from development by surrounding
Pachaug State Forest, is, of course, not comparable in size or
isolation to this vast, roadless north country of which Jaques
speaks. Yet the experience she describes could easily be repeated

on the Pachaug River, where you will often find yourself in wild country.

The landscape changes dramatically as you go south to the coast for a visit to Rocky Neck Park in East Lyme in Connecticut's most celebrated resort area. For wildlife watchers, the best time to visit the southeastern coast of Connecticut is in the spring or fall, when a quiet walk along the beach in search of shorebirds is an especially enjoyable experience.

PACHAUG STATE FOREST

One of the most beautiful, unspoiled areas in Connecticut lies within the boundaries of Pachaug State Forest, the state's largest forest, with headquarters in Voluntown. Covering almost 24,000 acres, the forest includes a favorite canoeing stream (the Pachaug River), lakes and ponds that provide excellent fishing, thirty-five miles of marked hiking trails, fifty-eight campsites, thirty miles of gravel automobile roads, miles of horseback riding trails, and many picnic sites scattered throughout the forest. Pachaug State Forest also contains a unique natural area, a white-cedar swamp where the great rhododendron grows wild and in glorious profusion. It is one of very few such areas to be found in New England.

Once the home of the Narragansett, Pequot, and Mohegan Native American tribes, this region was not settled by Europeans until the early 1700s. A tract of land six miles square was granted to the veterans of the Indian Wars. The central part of this area became known as "Volunteers Town," or Voluntown, and was incorporated in 1721. The entire area was farmed and, with the abundant waterpower, many small mills were constructed. Mills for spinning cotton yarn were followed in later years by those for weaving cotton cloth. However, with the development of modern systems of transportation and improved production methods, industrial development moved away from eastern Connecticut. Today there are scattered farms and small villages and, in this inland area, a haven for those who enjoy the natural world and outdoor activities.

Pachaug State Forest began with a land purchase in Voluntown in 1928. Today, as you walk through this healthy forest, it is hard to imagine that in the 1920s this forest region was one of the most devastated parts of New England. Trees had been cut again and again without any regard for reforestation, and repeated fires had wreaked more havoc. Extensive plantations of conifers, some of which have now been growing over fifty years, have helped to restore the forest and attract wildlife. Deer, foxes, raccoons, rabbits, squirrels, pheasants, grouse, and woodcocks may be found here.

To reach the Rhododendron Sanctuary from the center of Voluntown, drive one mile north on State 49. Turn left at the "Forest Headquarters" sign and continue on Headquarters Road to the Mount Misery Recreation Area. There are parking places by a field. To the east of the parking area, a section of the Nehantic Trail winds through the Rhododendron Sanctuary.

This is one walk that you should plan to do between June 15 and July 15. The shrubs generally reach full bloom around July 4. Entering this white-cedar and hemlock swamp forest and seeing for the first time the delicate pink blossoms of this wild rhododendron is an experience unlike any other in Connecticut and one you will never forget. The shrubs tower over your head on either side of the narrow trail, the buds a deeper shade of pink than the blossoms. Tall trunks of white-cedar trees rise from the forest floor, their evergreen crowns filtering the sunlight so that you walk through a cool green world. Shafts of sunlight fall on the pink blossoms and illumine the dark woods. Here, too, grow tall ferns such as the royal fern and the ostrich fern. Sphagnum moss and bog plants like sundews, goldthread, and bearberry carpet the ground. In this forest, one feels miles away from civilization. The only sounds I heard were the chattering of a red squirrel and the call of a bird I could not identify. The trail circles back to the road just north of where you left your car.

Mount Misery Campground has twenty-two wooded sites available on a first-come, first-served basis. Facilities include fireplaces, drinking water, and chemical toilets. There is stream fishing in Mount Misery Brook.

The Mount Misery Area serves as a good base camp for hikers. From here you can hike south on the Nehantic Trail to Green Falls Pond, where there is another campground with eighteen wooded sites. Green Falls Pond, with its trout, small islands, and wooded shores lined with rock ledges is a fishing, swimming, and boating paradise. However, the pond is also accessible by auto via Green Falls Road off State 138, so the area may be crowded on summer weekends. Car-top boats may be launched at the pond.

You can also hike north on the Nehantic Trail to Hopeville Pond State Park for swimming and camping. The total distance of this trail is about fourteen miles.

From Mount Misery Campground, you can gain access to the Pachaug Trail, which joins the Nehantic Trail east of Headquarters Road near the CCC Youth Area. You can hike for thirty miles on the Pachaug Trail through rugged country, passing streams, ponds, and rock formations, and continue on into the Arcadia Management Area of southwestern Rhode Island, all without leaving state-owned land. It is indeed fortunate that two relatively small and developed states have had the foresight to preserve this large area from development. It benefits man, by providing endless opportunities for outdoor recreation and nature study, and wildlife, by offering an almost continuous tract of land where commercial development does not intrude.

Maps of the recreation areas and trails in Pachaug State Forest are available from the State Parks Division of the Department of Environmental Protection. The Mount Misery Area is part of the Herman Haupt Chapman Management Area. On May 21, 1966, 2,000 acres of Pachaug State Forest were dedicated as a memorial to Chapman, a professor at the Yale School of Forestry, for his interest in the preservation of Connecticut's natural resources.

Just south of the "Forest Headquarters" sign on State 49 is the state boat-launching area, which is restricted to fishing and the launching of boats on the Pachaug River. There is space for parking, and those who use a wheelchair will find a ramp and fishing platform overlooking the river. Largemouth bass and 'yellow perch are the species most often caught here.

A gentle, copper-colored ribbon of water, the Pachaug River winds its way through the forest. Part of a chain of lakes and ponds, the river flows for many miles through wild country

Black ducks live in marshes, lakes, streams, coastal mudflats, and estuaries

and small villages. From the launching area you can canoe downstream into Beachdale Pond, a shallow body of water with extensive marshes, where you can have a good chance of seeing painted turtles. You can also canoe upstream on the Pachaug, past a private campground, Nature's Campsites, which has large wooded sites, some of them right along the river. Canoe rentals are available to campers. In all, an 11.5-mile canoe trip is possible on the Pachaug River through the chain of lakes and ponds from Doaneville Pond off State 138 through Glasgo Pond, Pachaug Pond, Hopeville Pond, and Ashland Pond, where the Pachaug joins the Quinebaug River, another good flat-water canoeing stream. Wildlife you might see on a canoe trip include black ducks, wood ducks, and kingfishers. Toward evening you might see signs of beaver activity or catch a glimpse of a deer coming to the edge of the river or a pond to drink.

Where: The entrance to Pachaug State Forest (Mount Misery Area and State Forest Headquarters) is one mile north of the center of Voluntown on State 49.

Hours: Recreation areas in Pachaug State Forest are open for day use year-round, as conditions permit, from 8:00 A.M. to sunset. The official camping season begins on April 15 and ends September 30. Check with Forest Headquarters if you want to camp before or after these dates.

Admission: At Green Falls Pond, there is a charge for parking, weekends and holidays during the summer season. A daily fee is also charged for camping permits.

Best time to visit: The Rhododendron Sanctuary should be visited between June 15 and July 15 in order to see the shrubs in bloom. Otherwise, any season, except during hunting season, is a good time for exploring this vast state forest.

Activities: Hiking, viewing unique natural delights, canoeing, camping, fishing, horseback riding, cross-country skiing, snowshoeing, dog-sled racing.

Concessions: At nearby Hopeville Pond State Park in Griswold,

North American Canoe Tours rents canoes at Hopeville Pond, which is actually part of the Pachaug River that has been widened for a distance of three miles. Canoes are available from Memorial Day through mid-June, weekends only, and mid-June to Labor Day, daily.

Pets: Pets on a leash are allowed on state-forest trails and in picnic areas. They are also allowed at the three campgrounds, where they are limited to one per campsite and must be on a leash not to exceed seven feet in length. Dogs must have proof of rabies vaccination.

Other: In addition to the campgrounds at Green Falls Pond and in the Mount Misery Area, there is Frog Hollow Horse Camp, designed specifically for equestrian use. The campground has eighteen semiwooded sites, which are available on a first-come, first-served basis. The season extends from April 15 through Thanksgiving.

Besides the state campgrounds and Nature's Campsites, open May 1 to October 15, another private campground in Voluntown that will appeal to those who enjoy nature-related activities is Ye Olde Countryside Campground, also open from May 1 to October 15, with unusually large sites shaded by pines and oaks. Some sites have rock ledges, and many overlook the pond, where campers enjoy fishing and swimming.

For more information:

Pachaug State Forest, P.O. Box 5, Voluntown, CT 06384; 203-376-4075.

State Parks Division, Department of Environmental Protection, 79 Elm Street, Hartford, CT 06106-5127; 203-566-2304 (for maps and general information on state camping areas).

Nature's Campsites, Route 49-N, Voluntown, CT 06384; 203-376-4203.

Ye Olde Countryside Campground, Box 80B, Voluntown, CT 06384; 203-376-0029.

North American Canoe Tours, Inc., 65 Black Point Road, Niantic, CT 06357; 203-739-0791.

ROCKY NECK STATE PARK

A white sand beach on Long Island Sound brings hundreds of visitors to Rocky Neck State Park in East Lyme each summer. The warm, clear water and gently sloping beach, along with campsites within walking distance of the beach, make the park a favorite destination for family vacations. Since the park is crowded in summer, the best times for nature and bird walks are in spring, fall, and even winter.

That this fine recreatonal area was set aside as a public park was due to the foresight of a few conservationists led by Henry Graves and Albert M. Turner, who in 1931 used their own personal funds to hold the land until they were recompensed by the state legislature.

The 561-acre park is bounded on the west by Four Mile River, a tidal river, and on the east by a broad salt marsh. The entrance road runs along the border of the marsh, and if you drive this road in spring or fall, you have a good chance of seeing great blue herons, black ducks, green-winged teal, and mallards. Rocky Neck State Park is also a good place to see ospreys, which visit there in early summer.

Bride Brook also flows through the park, and in March and April high spring tides allow great schools of alewives (herring) to swim into Bride Brook on a journey to their inland spawning grounds. There is a crabbing and handicapped-accessible fishing area on the brook where the entrance road crosses the stream, just before the first parking area.

The attractive campground is located near the park entrance. Five separate areas, named after shorebirds, have a total of 169 wooded and open sites. There are separate tenting areas near a nature center. Facilities include modern rest rooms with showers. Individual fireplaces are not provided. Those who bring bicycles will find a bikeway that connects the camping area with the park road near the first parking area.

A large pavilion of native fieldstone, built mostly by hand during the 1930s, overlooks the beach and a stone fishing jetty. Pillars supporting the pavilion were cut from trees in each of the state parks and state forests. On cool or rainy days, picnickers and campers gather around the pavilion's large fireplaces.

Hiking trails in the park consist of a main circular trail marked with white blazes and side trails marked with yellow blazes that lead to places with intriguing names like Baker's Cave, Tony's Nose, and Shipyard. Hikers should park in the first large parking area to the right of the entrance. Here trail maps are available. The trail starts at a white blaze near the far corner of the lot and crosses a marsh, where you may see ducks. Beyond the marsh, you enter woods where, depending on the season, you may find mountain laurel in bloom or ripe blueberries. The trail affords views of the Four Mile River and Long Island Sound before ending at the beach.

Saltwater fishing is a popular pastime either from the jetty or the beach. Depending on the time of year, you can fish for mackerel, striped bass, or flounder.

Where: Take exit 72 off I-95 and follow the signs east to the park, which is located off State 156 in East Lyme.

Hours: Open for day use year-round as conditions permit from 8:00 A.M. to sunset. The camping season extends from April 15 to September 30. However, check first with the State Parks Division if you want to camp before Memorial Day or after Labor Day.

Admission: There is a daily parking fee during the summer season. A fee is also charged weekends only from April 15 through Memorial Day, and again from Labor Day through the end of September. A nightly fee is charged for each campsite.

Best time to visit: Spring, fall, and winter are the best times as the park is crowded in summer.

Activities: Swimming, scuba diving, hiking, camping, bird-watching, picnicking, bicycling, saltwater fishing, interpretive programs, and cross-country skiing. Picnicking, camping, and fishing facilities are accessible to the handicapped.

Concessions: During the summer months a food concession operates and is handicapped accessible.

Pets: Not allowed on the beach or in the camping area.

For more information:

Rocky Neck State Park, Box 676, Niantic, CT 06357; 203-739-5471.

State Parks Division, Department of Environmental Protection, 79 Elm Street, Hartford, CT 06106-5127; 203-566-2304.

RHODE ISLAND

6

Inland

Our village life would stagnate
if it were not for the unexplored forests
and meadows which surround it.
We need the tonic of wilderness. . . .

— Henry David Thoreau
Walden

Not only is Rhode Island the smallest state, but its population density is exceeded only by that of New Jersey. These facts help explain the pressures for development that threaten the state's natural areas. Nevertheless, most citizens of Rhode Island live entirely in cities, and the western part of the state remains a rural area with forests, glacial bogs, streams, ponds, and freshwater swamps that provide a home for wildlife as well as a refuge for people—places where you can hike or swim or paddle a canoe and hear only the sounds of birds or the call of a bullfrog from a forested swamp.

Fortunately, a coalition of state and private organizations is working to protect Rhode Island's natural areas. Large tracts of land have been set aside as state parks and forests. In addition, three private organizations—the Audubon Society of Rhode Island, the Heritage Trust of Rhode Island, and The Nature Conservancy—are working together along with local private land trusts for the purpose of protecting land and the wildlife and plant life found there. The Audubon Society of Rhode Island manages more than 6,500 acres, tracts of land that are important because they provide critical habitat or offer special natural features. The Heritage Trust of Rhode Island holds both natural areas and historical sites, and The Nature Conservancy owns or controls about 800 acres in eight wildlife habitat preserves for endangered species in Rhode Island.

Preserving the forests and meadows while protecting the ponds and streams of interior Rhode Island will ensure that the "tonic of wilderness" will always be there.

CASIMIR PULASKI MEMORIAL STATE PARK

Situated in northwestern Rhode Island, Casimir Pulaski Memorial State Park, surrounded by 3,200 acres of the George Washington Management Area, is one of Rhode Island's most picturesque state parks. Located off US 44 just east of the Rhode Island state line, the park attracts many visitors in the summer with its long sandy beach and inviting warm-water swimming and fishing in Peck Pond. However, on a Sunday afternoon in August, I did not find the park overly crowded. There was plenty of space to enjoy a swim and picnic, and while hiking around the pond, I met only two other persons. What makes this park attractive in addition to the pond is the rolling hilly terrain with rocks and ledges, fragrant pine woods, and ground carpeted with ferns, wintergreen, and blueberries.

Following the trail around the edge of the pond, I came upon several quiet fishing spots. One was a broad rock ledge that

A pair of wood ducks check out a possible home

reached to the water's edge. Kids love to fish here and enjoy the thrill of a tug on the line even if it turns out to be only a sunfish.

For a longer hike, a trail leads east and in about a quarter-mile connects with the Walkabout Trail in the George Washington Management Area. This trail actually consists of three overlapping loop trails, on which you can walk from two to eight miles. Trail maps are available from the Forestry Headquarters in Chepachet. New Englanders can thank Australia for this fine hiking trail. In 1965, while an Australian ship, the *Perth*, was in dry dock in Newport, her crew volunteered their services to build a hiking trail.

The eight-mile loop takes you through a forest of magnificent hemlocks and along an earthen dam built to create a marsh. Here nesting boxes have been put out to attract wood ducks. In addition to the colorful ducks, you may see muskrats, which also inhabit this marsh.

In about five miles, you come to Bowdish Reservoir and the George Washington Management Area Campground, with forty-five sites and two shelters in a wooded area overlooking the lake. The camping area, also accessible from US 44, is heavily used by those who come to swim, launch boats, and fish for large-mouth bass, yellow perch, and pickerel. Water-based recreation, including waterskiing, is heavy on the reservoir during the summer months, and the southwestern end has a good deal of private development.

The creation of Bowdish Reservoir unfortunately destroyed a large bog. Today the only remnants of this bog are a few floating islands, which still support some rare bog plants and sundews. Although you won't find solitude here, the reservoir is still a good destination for an enjoyable canoe trip in spring and fall. Paddle along the eastern shore and you'll find plenty of places to go ashore in the George Washington Management Area. However, the islands are in the center of the reservoir, and if there is wind, sizable waves can build up on this rather large body of water. Use caution when paddling out into open water.

A sunfish strikes the lure

Continuing the loop hike will take you through more groves of hemlock and along the shore of Wilbur Pond back to your starting point and the side trail back to Peck Pond. During this hike you have a good chance of spotting woodland songbirds, such as thrushes, flycatchers, and warblers. You may also hear the familiar call of the quail, or "bobwhite," or, in spring, listen to the drumming of the ruffed grouse. Deer, raccoons, rabbits, and squirrels also inhabit these woods.

Where: Casimir Pulaski Memorial State Park in West Glocester is reached via a left turn on Pulaski Road, just over the state line from Connecticut, on US 44 east. Turn at the sign for "Pulaski Recreation Area."

The George Washington Management Camping Area is also off US 44, two miles east of the Connecticut state line.

Hours: Pulaski Memorial State Park is open for day use from 5:00 A.M. until one-half hour after sunset, year-round.

Camping is available in the George Washington Management Area from April 8 to October 15. Permits are issued by the park ranger on a first-come, first-served basis.

Admission: During the summer season, a parking fee is charged at Pulaski Memorial State Park. There is also a nightly fee for camping permits.

Best time to visit: Spring and fall for hiking, camping, canoeing, and bird-watching. Although the park may be crowded in summer, it is still an enjoyable place for a picnic and swimming. In the winter the park is open for ice skating and cross-country skiing.

Activities: In both Pulaski Memorial State Park and George Washington Camping Area — swimming, hiking, picnicking, fishing, bird-watching, and cross-country skiing. George Washington Camping Area, in addition to camping, has a boat-launching area. In winter, Peck Pond in Pulaski Memorial State Park offers skating. During the summer season, lifeguards are on duty and park rangers are available to answer questions.

Concessions: None.

Facilities: Facilities at Pulaski Memorial State Park include bathhouses, rest rooms, and a covered picnic pavilion.

Pets: Pets are not allowed on the beach or in the camping area. Otherwise, pets on a leash are permitted.

For more information:

Rhode Island Department of Environmental Management, Division of Parks and Recreation, 2321 Hartford Avenue, Johnston, RI 02919; 401-277-2632.

George Washington Management Area, 2185 Putnam Pike, Chepachet, RI 02814; 401-568-2013.

POWDER MILL LEDGES WILDLIFE REFUGE

Powder Mill Ledges Refuge, a wildlife sanctuary of the Audubon Society of Rhode Island, covers eighty-one acres and is situated just off busy US 44 in Smithfield. The Audubon Society headquarters is also located here.

Founded in 1897, the Audubon Society of Rhode Island, an independent state organization, even in its earliest years recognized the importance of conservation of natural habitats to protect birds and other wildlife and plants. Today the society manages more than 6,500 acres in Rhode Island, retaining most of the woodlands and wetlands in their natural state for wildlife habitat and/or watershed protection. Seven of the sixty-five properties operate as education centers, with groomed trails and programs and walks led by professional naturalists. Powder Mill Ledges Wildlife Refuge is one of the properties that has been developed for public use.

This upland woodland refuge is notable for its stands of northern red oak, white pine, and pitch pine and for its small pond and wetlands, which attract many species of wildlife. For those who walk its trails, it is a refuge from the spreading commercial and residential development along heavily traveled US 44.

The land has a long history of use. The original forest was cut to provide lumber for homes, carriages, and ships. In the 1800s it was part of a dairy farm, and cows grazed on what was then a treeless hillside pasture. When you walk the trails today, you will see the old stone walls that were part of the farm. The refuge takes its name from a powder mill that was built in the area, although the exact location remains unknown. By the early 1900s, the land was already returning to forest. Many species of wildflowers were recorded, and the pond attracted ducks and herons.

The refuge features three loops of trails. Before starting out to walk the trails, stop at the headquarters building to register and pick up a trail map and a guide to the orange loop trail. The building also houses the Hathaway Library of Natural History and an excellent book and gift shop. Available for purchase for a small fee is a "Properties Map," which will serve as a guide to the other Audubon refuges open to the public. It also includes a chart listing all the Audubon Society of Rhode Island properties and their features.

The entrance to the orange marked trail is near the headquarters building. The sound of traffic fades as you enter a section of the woodland where you pass a sugar maple, quaking aspens, red maples, and red oaks. Along the edge of a field, nesting boxes for tree swallows and eastern bluebirds crown the fence posts.

Continuing along the trail, you reach a forested swamp, which sits in a depression formed by the last glacier. This swamp is undergoing the process of natural succession: what was once open water evolved into a marsh, and then a shrub swamp, before it became a forested swamp. Most of the trees here are red maples. Many kinds of birds are attracted to this area—more than 150 species have been recorded in the refuge. The swamp and small pond are also home to a variety of frogs, such as wood and green frogs, turtles, and aquatic insects. As I approached the pond, I heard the calls of bullfrogs and saw painted turtles sunning themselves on a partly submerged log. A walk by the pond may even reward you with the sight of a great blue heron or a muskrat.

Before passing through a high stone wall built by farmers long ago, look for three kinds of ferns on the left: cinnamon fern, sensitive fern, and lady fern. The refuge is also a good place to test your wildflower identification skills. In late spring and early summer, many plants that have thrived here since the early days of this century are in bloom. See if you can spot jack-in-the-pulpit, pipsissewa, downy rattlesnake plantain, pink lady's slipper, Indian cucumber root, false Solomon's seal, true Solomon's seal, wild geranium, and Turk's-cap lilies.

The trail then continues uphill through a fragrant white-pine forest. After grazing ended on this hillside pasture, pine seedlings began to take over the field. Some large hardwoods have also grown up, but it is the sweet scent of the pine woods that you will remember.

The fields of the refuge, which provide food for many seed-eating birds and mammals, including mice and woodchucks, are mowed only once every two years. Goldenrod, joe-pye weed, sensitive fern, and wetland grasses grow here. Wildlife food patches, such as rye grass and sunflowers, have been planted to supplement the winter food supply within the refuge. Song sparrows and other field species would lose their habitat if the fields were allowed to return to forest.

Despite human intrusion in the form of a shopping center bordering the refuge, spring peepers and American toads still use the wetland at the end of the parking area, and their calls can be heard on a spring evening. Trees planted along the boundary line to act as a buffer provide additional habitat for such birds as catbirds, mockingbirds, and robins.

Back at the headquarters building, a bird-feeding area with a bird blind nearby lets photographers and bird-watchers view the birds without disturbing them. Along the side of the building, next to the bird blind, is a butterfly garden with flowers that provide nectar for butterflies to feed on as well as plants that certain caterpillars need for food.

This sanctuary demonstrates how home owners can make even a small property more hospitable to wildlife by planting shrubs and trees for cover and food and by replacing part of the lawn with a section of wildflowers and grasses. Even on a very small lot, you can plant a butterfly garden, and put out bird feeders in winter to supplement the natural supply of food.

Where: From exit 7B on I-295, drive west one mile to US 44, then 0.1 mile south on State 5. The headquarters building and parking lot at 12 Sanderson Road in Smithfield will be on your left after you make the turn at this busy intersection.

Hours: Trails are open from dawn to dusk. The headquarters building, with its library and book and gift shop, is open from 9:00 A.M. to 5:00 P.M. weekdays and from 8:00 A.M. to 6:00 P.M. on weekends.

Admission: A nominal fee may be charged to defray maintenance costs. Fees are charged for special programs, but members of the Audubon Society of Rhode Island can attend programs at reduced rates.

Best time to visit: Spring and fall to see birds, late spring and early summer for wildflowers, winter for cross-country skiing.

Activities: Nature walks to observe and learn about wildlife, including bird-watching, and about wildflowers and other plants. (A self-guided tour on one of the trails can be used to learn to identify many species of plants and trees.) Photographing plants, birds, and animals. In winter snow, cross-country skiing and snowshoeing. Exhibits, films, educational programs, and walks led by professional naturalists.

Pets: Not allowed.

Other: Picnicking is not allowed here. Nearby Pulaski Memorial State Park is a good place to have your lunch.

For more information:

Audubon Society of Rhode Island, 12 Sanderson Road (Route 5), Smithfield, RI 02917-2606; 401-231-6444.

ARCADIA MANAGEMENT AREA

Located north of Hope Valley in the southwestern part of Rhode Island, the Arcadia Management Area, which encompasses 14,000 acres of state-owned land, is one of the largest remaining natural areas in this smallest state in the Northeast. Visitors will find recreation areas at Beach Pond and Browning Mill Pond (also known as Arcadia Park), miles of hiking trails, several ponds, trout streams, and delightful views.

You can reach this area easily from State 165, which traverses the heart of the state forest. Beach Pond, a large body of water that stretches across the state line into Connecticut, is on State 165. The parking area is in Exeter, Rhode Island. Beach Pond Recreation Area shares a two-mile-long beach with Pachaug State Forest in Connecticut. The long sandy beach and clear water make this a popular spot for swimming and boating, and it is likely to be crowded during the summer. One of Rhode Island's most memorable hiking trails, the Hemlock Ledges Trail, which is part of the Tippecansett Trail, begins at the beach parking area and follows along the shore of the pond. From the summit of the ledges, you see all of Beach Pond.

As you head east on State 165, the landscape varies from gently rolling hills to level stretches of scrub oak and pine reminiscent of Cape Cod. A right turn on Arcadia Road will take you to the Browning Mill Pond Recreation Area. Here on a warm summer day, the crescent-shaped beach is an ideal destination. The sand is soft, the water is warm and shallow, and there is a safe, roped-off wading area for children. Fishing for pickerel and smallmouth and largemouth bass is a favorite pastime.

The picnic area at Browning Mill Pond is outstanding. Some of the tables are scattered along the shore of the pond and on a wooded peninsula, while others are close to Roaring Brook or in a quiet expanse beneath tall trees. Many sites have fireplaces. Just beyond the beach, in the upper picnic area near the pavilion, Roaring Brook cascades through the woods, dropping into clear, shallow pools that delight children. The covered picnic pavilion is available for group use by reservation only.

On a warm weekday in mid-July, I found the beach and picnic areas uncrowded. Most of the swimmers had opted for the larger beach and deeper water at Beach Pond. In a summer of budget cuts, there was some evidence of maintenance work left undone and lack of staff. No lifeguard was on duty at the beach, but despite these problems — which, hopefully, will be remedied in future years — Arcadia Park remained an enchanting place for families with young children. I found my favorite picnic site unoccupied. Situated on a point of land extending into the pond, it captures a restful view and the shade of tall pine trees. I ate lunch while cooling my feet in the water and enjoying the breeze.

Since I was last in Arcadia Park, a small flock of Canada geese had taken up residence at the pond. Depending on how you feel about sharing a swimming beach with geese, this can be viewed as either a positive or a negative feature; but watching them swim in the shallow water among the water lilies, I could not help but feel that they belonged here.

The Arcadia Management Area offers thirty miles of hiking trails that are maintained by the Narragansett Chapter of the Appalachian Mountain Club. Views and wildlife are abundant. Hikers report seeing deer, foxes, otter, beaver, raccoons, and coyotes.

After lunch I hiked a section of the Arcadia Trail that begins at the Dawley State Park Picnic Area off State 3 and traverses a wooded area with mature stands of beech trees before it reaches Arcadia Park and follows the shore of Browning Mill Pond. Along the shore of the pond, tall shrubs border the trail. In July, I found the fragrant pink blossoms of wild honeysuckle and a few ripe high-bush blueberries. Earlier in the season, mountain laurel had been in bloom. Tall oaks, maples, hickories, and white pine are the predominant trees. Ferns and club mosses carpet the ground. Large boulders are scattered about the hilly terrain, and stone walls testify that this was once farming country.

Backpack camping is available by permit only at the Stepstone Falls Camping Area, where the Falls River flows over a series of wide, flat rocks that resemble giant steps. The four campsites are available on a first-come, first-served basis. The camping area is located between the Tippecansett and Ben Utter Trails.

A special campground for persons with horses is located on Escoheag Hill Road, north of State 165. Permits are issued at the area with a four-night maximum stay allowed.

The Mount Tom Trail begins along State 165 about 2.5 miles west of State 3. In less than one mile it reaches a parking area on the Wood River, a favorite with trout fishermen and canoeists. The trail then passes through a pine forest planted after a fire destroyed over 7,000 acres of forestland in 1951. The pines now serve as a resting area for warblers during migration periods. In a little more than two miles from the start of this hike, the trail ascends to rock ledges from which there is a panoramic view of the forested valleys below. The trail continues on to the forested summit, but the views are best from the ledges.

A brochure describing the hiking trails is available from the Department of Environmental Management. Many of the trails in the Arcadia Management Area are linked to trails in Pachaug State Forest in Connecticut. For hikers and wildlife watchers, this means that an area of more than 36,000 acres has been set aside for the benefit of man and wildlife, an area where maintaining the natural environment and protecting the quality of natural resources are the primary goals.

Where: From Voluntown, Connecticut, drive east on State 165. Beach Pond Recreation Area is on State 165. Parking is on the left just over the Rhode Island border.

To reach the Browning Mill Pond Recreation Area, continue driving east on State 165. About six miles from the Rhode Island state line, and shortly after passing a sign and entrance road on the left for the Arcadia Management Headquarters, turn right on an unmarked road known as Arcadia Road. Although there was no road or park sign when I was there, it is the only wide paved road running south from State 165. If you miss the turn, you will reach the intersection of State 3 after one mile. By turning around and going west on State 165, you can then take your first left. Parking for the Browning Mill Pond Recreation Area will be on your right. From there it is a short walk down the hill to the pond and beach.

Hours: The Arcadia Management Area is open for day use from 5:00 A.M. until one hour after sunset. Pond and stream fishing is allowed when the area is closed for other activities.

Permits for backpack camping must be obtained in person. During the summer season, the park office at Browning Mill Pond is normally open daily from 8:30 A.M. to 4:00 P.M. At other times permits will be issued from the Division of Forest Environment Headquarters on Arcadia Road, weekdays only, from 8:30 A.M. to 4:00 P.M.

Admission: A fee is charged for parking at the Beach Pond Recreation Area during the summer season. No fee for use of the Browning Mill Pond Recreation Area. Campers pay a fee for permits to camp at the Stepstone Falls Backpack Camping Area and at Legrand G. Reynolds Horsemen's Camping Area on Escoheag Hill Road.

Best time to visit: Any time of year is a good time to explore the Arcadia Management Area. With the exception of Beach Pond on summer weekends, the area is not likely to be overcrowded. Spring, during the warbler migration, and fall foliage season are special times to visit this area. Cross-country skiers will find weekdays best for winter nature walks because snowmobiling is allowed on state forest roads and use may be heavy on weekends.

Activities: Hiking, swimming, picnicking, fishing, horseback riding, backpack and horsemen's camping, cross-country skiing, and snowmobiling.

Concessions: None.

Pets: No dogs are allowed on beaches or in camping areas. Dogs on a leash, not more than twenty-five feet long, are allowed in picnic areas and on trails.

Other: For family camping, two private campgrounds are located in West Greenwich, surrounded by acres of state forest lands for hiking, swimming, and boating. Oak Embers Campground, open from February to December, has sixty shaded sites for tents and RVs, several Adirondack-style shelters, a camp store, swimming pool, and game room. Pine Valley R.V. Campground, open year-round, has fifty tent sites and twenty RV sites located in a field and wooded area with a store, swimming pool, and recreation hall.

For more information:

Rhode Island Department of Environmental Management, Division of Forest Environment, Arcadia Headquarters, RFD 1, Box 55, Hope Valley, RI 02832; 401-539-2356.

Legrand G. Reynolds Horsemen's Camping Area, 260 Arcadia Road, Hope Valley, RI 02832; 401-539-2356 or 277-1157.

Oak Embers Campground, Escoheag Hill Road, West Greenwich, RI 02817; 401-397-4042.

Pine Valley R.V. Campground, 64 Bailey Road, West Greenwich, RI 02817; 401-397-7972 or 392-3320. In Connecticut, 203-564-7587.

7

The Coast

There is nothing so small, nothing so great,
That it does not respond to those celestial spring days,
and give the pendulum of life a fresh start.

—John Burroughs
Birds and Poets

It was in the spring that I spent a day at Ninigret Conservation Area, on a day when the long sandy beach belonged to the birds and to those who came to watch them. No place in Rhode Island is more than twenty-five miles from the sea. Unlike Connecticut, where the coast is sheltered by the long arm of Long Island, Rhode Island's coast faces the open Atlantic, but along its shores are salt ponds and marshes protected from the open ocean by barrier beaches. The ponds serve as a nursery and feeding ground for a great variety of birds and shellfish, and protected coastal ponds and marshes serve as a refuge for birds and waterfowl during seasonal migrations.

Narragansett Bay cuts deeply into the land. With its many

islands, coves, and channels, it invites endless exploration both by land and by sea.

I hope that the following pages will serve as an introduction to the natural wonders of coastal Rhode Island. Those who spend time here will discover many other special places.

NINIGRET NATIONAL WILDLIFE REFUGE AND CONSERVATION AREA

The Ninigret National Wildlife Refuge occupies a 404-acre tract of coastal plain near Charlestown. It borders the northern end of Ninigret Pond, which is four miles long and half a mile wide at its broadest point. The Ninigret Conservation Area is a barrier beach more than two miles long. No vehicles are allowed in the refuge, and the only access to the Conservation Area is via East Beach Road. When you reach the beach, turn left, drive past some cottages, and you will see the entrance signs and parking area for Ninigret Conservation Area. From here you have access to the shore of Ninigret Pond and the barrier beach. Visit this area in fall or spring because in summer the beach attracts crowds and the parking lot is closed when it is filled to capacity.

On a cool day in mid-May when the sun was having a hard time breaking through the clouds, I found an almost deserted beach. Only two other persons were braving the cool breeze and threat of showers to walk beside the waves. Just as I reached the ocean, the sun broke through the clouds, illuminating everything with a magical light that lasted several moments. A small flock of terns had alighted on the beach, and a lone piping plover was working the edge of the incoming waves. Ducks flew overhead, and a great black-backed gull appeared to be the sentinel of the beach. I could see Block Island twelve miles away and a couple of fishing boats.

You can walk this beach for a distance of over two miles

A big bite for a small tern

as far as the Charlestown Breachway, which connects Ninigret
Pond with the Atlantic Ocean. During a walk along this beach in
spring or fall, you are likely to see sandpipers, plovers, and
willets feeding at the edge of the tide, and ducks, including
canvasbacks and goldeneyes, riding the waves offshore. On a
nice day, you can enjoy the sunshine, the ocean, and the birds,
and the only sounds you are apt to hear are the waves breaking on
the beach and the cry of gulls overhead.

From the parking area, it is just a few steps to the shore of
Ninigret Pond, the largest in a string of ponds along the southern
Rhode Island shore. Sign boards inform the visitor that this salt
pond is a rich environment that is both a nursery and a feeding
ground for shellfish, finfish, and birds. Because the salt water is
diluted with fresh water from streams and springs, the pond can
nourish brackish species like oysters as well as creatures of the

sea such as quahogs, soft-shelled clams, and flounder. Flounder lay their eggs in Ninigret Pond during the winter; the young hatch and remain in the pond feeding for two or three years. Aquatic vegetation flourishes in ponds like Ninigret, which has an average depth of only four feet. The plant nutrients provide a rich source of food for finfish and shellfish. Salt ponds play a vital role. In serving as nurseries, they supply the ocean with many varieties of fish. Ninigret Pond and adjoining Green Hill Pond supply Block Island Sound with as much as one-quarter of its winter flounder. The pond also attracts black ducks, which feed on the abundant eelgrass, and mallards, which nest along the banks each year. Mute swans also nest and raise their young along the edges of the pond.

In addition to hiking along the beach, you have a wide choice of other activities in the area. There are hiking trails within the federal refuge—a map is posted at Foster Cove off US 1—and you can also hike on Grassy Point, which is accessible from Ninigret Park off State 1A in Charlestown. Ninigret Park is a recreational park with a swimming pond, picnic grounds, ballfields, and tennis and basketball courts situated on 172 acres. The Frosty Drew Nature Center is also located in the park near the refuge entrance. It is open during the summer months and offers interpretive programs and nature-related activities for children. Trail maps and information can also be obtained there.

The checklist of bird species for the Ninigret National Wildlife Refuge, which includes satellite refuges at Trustom Pond, Sachuest Point, and Block Island, lists 289 species, practically all the species that are found in Rhode Island. Wading birds that have been seen at Ninigret Pond include the snowy egret, glossy ibis, great blue heron, green heron, and black-crowned night heron. In addition, many songbirds frequent the wooded areas of the refuge.

Forty species of mammals have been recorded, including

red and gray foxes, coyotes, woodchucks, white-tailed deer, and chipmunks.

Camping is available in three areas. Within Ninigret Conservation Area, located in two primitive areas with access by sand trail requiring four-wheel drive, are twenty sites for self-contained units only. You can also camp in the nearby Burlingame State Park in Charlestown. This 100-acre park, with frontage on the shore of Watchaug Pond, has a large camping area with 755 sites. Facilities include tables, fireplaces, and rest rooms with showers. The Charlestown Breachway has seventy-five sites for self-contained trailer units only.

Where: Ninigret Conservation Area is reached via East Beach Road, off US 1 in Charlestown.

Ninigret Park is off State 1A in Charlestown.

The entrance to Burlingame State Park is on US 1 in Charlestown.

Charlestown Breachway is off Charlestown Beach Road in Charlestown.

Hours: Ninigret Conservation Area and Ninigret Park are open daily year-round from sunrise to sunset. Camping is available in Ninigret Conservation Area, Burlingame State Park, and the Charlestown Breachway from April 15 to October 31.

Admission: A fee is charged for parking at Ninigret Conservation Area daily during the summer season, but weekends and holidays only during the off-season. There is a camping fee at each of the three areas.

Best time to visit: Spring and fall to hike the beach and trails. The area is crowded in summer.

Activities: At Ninigret Conservation Area there is hiking, wildlife watching, swimming (lifeguard on duty 10:00 A.M. to 6:00 P.M. during the summer), boating, fishing, and shellfishing (nonresident license required).

At Burlingame State Park there is camping, boating, fishing, and swimming in Watchaug Pond.

The Charlestown Breachway offers camping, a boat-launching ramp, saltwater fishing, and swimming.

The Frosty Drew Memorial Nature Center in Ninigret Park has displays and programs.

Concessions: None.

Pets: Not allowed.

For more information:

Rhode Island Department of Environmental Management, Division of Parks and Recreation, 2321 Hartford Avenue, Johnston, RI 02919; 401-277-2632.

Ninigret Conservation Area, 401-322-0450 (seasonal).

Burlingame State Park, 401-322-7994 or 322-7337.

Charlestown Breachway, 401-364-7000 (seasonal) or 322-8910.

Ninigret Park, 401-334-6244 or 364-7718.

Ninigret National Wildlife Refuge, Box 307, Charlestown, RI 02813; 401-364-9124.

TRUSTOM POND

The Trustom Pond Refuge, part of the Ninigret National Wildlife Refuge, was created when Ann Kenyon Morse donated her 350-acre coastal farm in South Kingston to the U.S. Fish and Wildlife Service in 1974. Trustom Pond, Rhode Island's largest protected coastal pond, attracts a great variety of birds and waterfowl that follow the Atlantic Flyway during spring and fall migrations. The shallow body of water surrounded by fields and scrub forest, with abundant berries and fruit from old orchards, provides a plentiful supply of food for wild creatures.

The farm's former barn has been converted into refuge

headquarters, and it's a good idea to stop here and pick up a trail map before hiking the circular trail, which offers good observation points on Trustom Pond.

In summer, you will find catbirds, robins, orioles, and thrashers feeding on wild cherries, blueberries, wild grapes, and blackberries. The trail leads to one of the narrow necks that extend into the pond. From this vantage point, you are likely to see the pond's resident flock of mute swans. Especially during spring and fall migrations, you may observe Canada geese, gulls, terns, loons, grebes, and ducks in Trustom Pond. In summer, visitors often spot egrets, herons, ospreys, and cormorants. The opposite shore of the pond is owned by the Rhode Island Audubon Society.

In winter, you can follow the trails on cross-country skis or snowshoes. Horned larks are often seen during the winter months. Such unusual species as murres, dovekies, shearwaters, and guillemots are sometimes blown into the area by coastal storms. You can also search for the tracks of the refuge's mammal population, which includes deer, red and gray foxes, and coyotes.

Where: Follow US 1 north from Charlestown to Moonstone Beach Road exit. Follow the road one mile and turn right on Matunuck School House Road. The entrance to the refuge is 0.7 mile on the left.

Hours: The refuge is open daily year-round from sunrise to sunset.

Admission: No charge.

Best time to visit: Spring, fall, and winter.

Activities: Bird-watching, photography, hiking, interpretive walks in summer. Cross-country skiing in winter. Trustom Pond and the acreage owned by the Rhode Island Audubon Society are jointly managed. Naturalists are on hand during the summer months to assist visitors and lead groups on nature walks.

Concessions: None.

Pets: Not allowed.

For more information:

Ninigret National Wildlife Refuge, Box 307, Charlestown, RI 02813; 401-364-9124.

BEAVERTAIL STATE PARK AND CONANICUT ISLAND

Beavertail State Park is located in the southwestern part of Conanicut Island at the tip of a nine-mile-long strip of land known as "the Beaver," which extends northward into Narragansett Bay from Rhode Island Sound. This beaver-shaped strip of land is connected to the main part of the island by a narrow neck of land at Mackerel Cove, where there is a small sand beach.

Conanicut Island, which you can reach by bridge from the mainland, was once the summer campground of the Narragansett Indians, who sold the island to settlers in 1657. Most of the early settlers were English Quakers who were sheep farmers. Jamestown has been a summer colony since 1872, and many of the island's early Victorian summer homes are still in use.

A drive along North Road to Conanicut Point takes you past the Jamestown Windmill, recently restored by the Jamestown Historical Society. Built in 1787 to grind corn, the mill was in operation until 1896. North Road, which follows an old Indian trail, was so named because on a clear night the North Star shines directly above the center of the road. Guided by its light, an Indian could easily travel the length of the island. At the northern tip of the island at Conanicut Point, stop to admire the view of Narragansett Bay and the Rhode Island coast.

Most of the land accessible for hiking, bicycle riding, or camping is located in the part of Conanicut Island that is south of Jamestown. Beavertail State Park encompasses 153 acres of land at the southern tip of the island. The rocky coast at Beavertail is the scenic equal of any spot on the southern New England shore. Fishermen come here in the early morning or evening to cast for striped bass. Others come to watch the surf endlessly breaking on the rocks. Storms launch showers of spray into the air all around the tail of the beaver.

Birdlife as well as marinelife is abundant in this coastal park. As many as 278 species of birds have been recorded on Conanicut Island. The manx shearwater, an oceanic bird usually found way out at sea, was first seen off Beavertail. Deer occasionally swim to the island, and rabbits and skunks are common.

Beavertail State Park is of historical interest because it is the site of Beavertail Lighthouse, the third-oldest continuously operating lighthouse in North America. The first navigational aid at Beavertail dates back to 1705. It consisted of an open pitch fire built and maintained by local Indians. In 1719 the first fog-warning device was installed. During heavy fog, a cannon was fired at regular intervals. In 1892, a fog bell operated by horses was installed. The present lighthouse dates back to 1856. Today it is fully automated with a light that is visible for seventeen miles.

GEOLOGIC HISTORY

This area is of geologic interest because the ledges, composed of hard metamorphic rock, are in contrast to the softer sedimentary rock found in most of the Narragansett basin. During the Ice Age the sedimentary rock was eroded by the glacier and its meltwater streams, but the hard bedrock was less affected. After the Ice Age ended and the sea level rose, these areas, including Beavertail Point, remained above the water level. Other areas of hard metamorphic rock became the islands of Narragansett Bay. If you examine the rocks, you will find scratches and fractures that were caused by the glacier that moved across New England some 20,000 years ago.

The state-park road circles the point. At intervals, footpaths descend from the parking areas to the rock ledges. Caution is advised when walking on the rock ledges since they can be extremely slippery.

During the winter, the ledges at Beavertail are a good location to see harbor seals, which seek shelter in the protected waters of Narragansett Bay. The best time to look for them is at low tide, when they often rest on the rock ledges. At high tide, they are usually offshore feeding on fish and shellfish. In winter, Beavertail Point is also a likely place to see ducks and geese.

The only camping area on Conanicut Island is in the Fort Getty Recreation Area and is maintained by the town of Jamestown. The recreation area is reached via Fort Getty Road off Beavertail Road, west of Mackerel Cove. The 125 sites, located on Fox Hill, have a panoramic view of Narragansett Bay. In summer, the surrounding meadows are a garden of wild roses, honeysuckle, and deep blue asters. There are 100 sites for trailers with water and electric hookups and a separate tenting area with 25 sites. There is little privacy between sites, but the location and the view are outstanding. Camping permits for all the sites are issued on a first-come, first-served basis. No reservations are taken, and during the summer season there are few vacant sites. Facilities include a boat ramp, a fishing dock, and modern rest rooms with showers. A picnic area on the shore has a covered pavilion, and you can swim at Mackerel Cove beach.

Where: Take State 138 east and south over the Jamestown Bridge to Conanicut Island and Jamestown. To reach Beavertail State Park, take Beavertail Road south from Jamestown about four miles to the park entrance.

Hours: Beavertail State Park is open sunrise to sunset year-round. Beavertail Lighthouse is open during the summer season for daily lectures and tours, Wednesday through Sunday. Call the park for information on tour schedules.

The Jamestown Windmill is open mid-June to mid-September, Saturday and Sunday, 1:00 to 4:00 P.M., and by appointment.

The camping season at the Fort Getty Recreation Area is May 22 through October 4.

Admission: No charge at Beavertail State Park. Camping fees are charged at the Fort Getty Recreation Area.

Best time to visit: Spring and fall are less crowded. Winter is the time to see harbor seals.

Activities: Fishing, hiking, picnicking, scenic overlooks, naturalist programs, and historic sites. Camping and boating at the Fort Getty Recreation Area. Swimming at Mackerel Cove.

Concessions: None.

Pets: Not allowed.

For more information:

Rhode Island Department of Environmental Management, Division of Parks and Recreation, 2321 Hartford Avenue, Johnston, RI 02919; 401-277-2632.

For information on Bevertail State Park or Beavertail Lighthouse, write to Goddard Memorial State Park, Ives Road, Warwick, RI 028128; 401-884-2010 or 401-423-9941 (seasonal at Beavertail State Park).

Fort Getty Recreation Area, P.O. Box 377, Jamestown, RI 02835; 401-423-7264 (seasonal).

For additional information on the Jamestown Windmill, contact the Jamestown Historical Society at 401-423-1798.

BAY ISLANDS PARK

One of Rhode Island's newer state parks, Bay Islands Park consists of 2,939 acres of land on the islands of Narragansett Bay. Once part of the harbor defense system, the islands' development into the park began in 1973 when the U.S. Navy turned over some of its property to the state. Prudence Island (containing North Prudence Island Park and South Prudence Island Park), Dutch Island, Hope Island (a bird rookery with restricted access), Patience Island, and Gould Island make up the park. The sheltered waters of Narragansett Bay are ideal for sailing and fishing, and Bay Islands Park ensures that the public will always have access to the bay and its islands.

Four of the islands — Dutch, Hope, Patience, and Gould — are virtually undeveloped. Three of the most unspoiled, ecologically fragile areas — North Prudence, Patience, and Hope — have special status as the Narragansett Bay Estuary Sanctuary. Access to Hope is restricted during nesting season from April through August, but you can land on the other islands and picnic, hike, study nature, and fish. Shellfishing is also permitted except on Hope. Nonresidents must obtain a license.

Prudence is the only inhabited island. Settled in the 1600s, the central part of the island still has both permanent and seasonal residents. However, the hectic pace of modern life hasn't touched this island, a sanctuary for white-tailed deer and birds, where roads are unpaved, and you are free to spend the day hiking, swimming, fishing, and bird-watching.

To get to the island, you can board the Prudence Ferry, which provides daily year-round service (except on Christmas and New Year's Day), from Church Street Wharf in Bristol. The ferry docks at Homestead, in the central part of the island. Since Prudence Island is only about seven miles long, bicycles are ideal for exploring. You can also bring a car to the island.

North of Homestead is North Prudence Park, which has nature and hiking trails, a boat dock, picnic tables, and a pit toilet.

To the south of Homestead is South Prudence Park, which welcomes those who come by private boat with its five public moorings, presently available for day use only. At the time of this writing, in July 1994, the campground at South Prudence

Island Park was temporarily closed with no date set for reopening. Other facilities available for day use include twelve picnic sites with tables and fireplaces, nature trails, a fishing dock, a saltwater beach area (no lifeguard on duty), portable toilets, an information booth, and a naturalist display area.

Where: Prudence Island can be reached by ferry service from Church Street Wharf in Bristol, Rhode Island. Church Street Wharf is off State Street, two miles north of the Mount Hope Bridge. Dutch, Patience, Gould, and Hope Islands are accessible by private boat only.

Hours: The islands in the Bay Islands Park system are open year-round for day use from 6:00 A.M. to 11:00 P.M. Access to Hope Island is restricted from April through August.

Admission: No fee is charged for access to these state-park areas. Check with the Prudence Ferry for a schedule and rates for transportation to and from the island.

Best time to visit: Late spring through October.

Activities: Fishing, shellfishing (except on Hope), hiking, biking, nature observation, picnicking, boating, and saltwater swimming, and seasonal naturalist programs on South Prudence.

Concessions: None.

Pets: Not allowed in the state-park areas. However, dogs on a leash are allowed on the Prudence Ferry.

For more information:

Rhode Island Department of Environmental Management, Division of Parks and Recreation, 2321 Hartford Avenue, Johnston, RI 02919; 401-277-2632.

Prudence Ferry, Inc., Church Street Wharf, Bristol, RI 02809; 401-253-9808.

BLITHEWOLD GARDENS AND ARBORETUM

To experience a place of natural beauty that man has had a hand in creating and preserving, visit Blithewold Gardens and

Arboretum in Bristol. Situated on thirty-three acres along the shore of Narragansett Bay, Blithewold was the forty-five-room summer home of Augustus Van Winkle, who had made his fortune in the coal industry. Built in 1908, the house and gardens, which include a rose garden, a water garden, and a rock garden, were designed by New York landscape architect John DeWolf.

Marjorie Van Winkle Lyon, daughter of the original owner, spent her summers at Blithewold until her death at the age of ninety-three. During her lifetime, she continued a family tradition of opening Blithewold to horticultural groups during the gardening season, and in her will she bequeathed Blithewold to the Heritage Trust of Rhode Island to ensure that visitors would always be able to enjoy the gardens and special beauty of this turn-of-the-century estate. Today the mansion, arboretum, and gardens are on the National Register of Historic Places.

In addition to native plants, you will find exotic species not usually found elsewhere in New England. One of these is a Chinese toon tree, the first known to flower in the United States. There is also a ninety-year-old giant sequoia, planted in 1911, which is now over eighty-five feet tall and the largest of its kind east of the Rocky Mountains. The tree grows about a foot a year. There are also Chinese cedars, ginkgoes, and a grove of bamboo believed to be the largest stand of bamboo in the Northeast. A brochure is available that describes the many species of trees you will see along a self-guided trail. You can also take a guided tour of the grounds and the seventeenth-century-style English manor house, which is furnished and decorated much as it was in the early 1900s. There is a gift shop in the carriage house. Bring a lunch to enjoy in one of the picnic areas on the lawns overlooking Narragansett Bay.

Where: From Providence, take exit 2 off I-195 in Massachusetts. Follow State 136 south for 8.5 miles. Turn right on Griswold Avenue. At the end of Griswold Avenue, turn left onto Ferry Road (State 114); Blithewold is a quarter-mile on the right.

Hours: The grounds are open year-round, 10:00 A.M. to 5:00 P.M. The mansion is open April to October, 10:00 A.M. to 4:00 P.M. and in December (4 to 23 and 26 to 30) when Christmas at Blithewold is celebrated. The mansion is usually closed Mondays and holidays. The gift shop is open daily, April to December.

Admission: A fee is charged for admission to the grounds and for tours of the mansion and grounds.

Best time to visit: April for spring bulb display, May through September to see the gardens in bloom.

Activities: Touring the mansion, gardens, arboretum; picnicking and special programs, including Concerts by the Bay (June to September), and horticultural and historical programs throughout the year; also, Christmas at Blithewold in December.

Concessions: None.

Pets: Not allowed.

For more information:

Blithewold Gardens and Arboretum, 101 Ferry Road, Bristol, RI 02809-0716; 401-253-2707.

Bibliography

Bolles, Frank. *At the North of Bearcamp Water.* Boston and New York: Houghton Mifflin Co., 1917.

Borland, Hal. *Beyond Your Doorstep: A Handbook to the Country.* New York: Alfred A. Knopf, 1962.

Bowen, Ezra. "The Million Dollar Fish," *Connecticut Magazine,* May 1994, pp. 39-44.

Burroughs, John. *Birds and Poets.* Vol. 3 of *The Writings of John Burroughs.* 19 vols. Boston and New York: Houghton Mifflin Co., 1877, 1895, and 1904.

Colbert, Edwin H. *The Great Dinosaur Hunters and Their Discoveries.* New York: Dover Publications, 1984.

Cooley, Susan D. *Country Walks in Connecticut: A Guide to the Nature Conservancy Preserves.* Boston: Appalachian Mountain Club and The Nature Conservancy, 1982.

Godin, Alfred J. *Wild Mammals of New England*. Field Guide Edition. Freeport, ME: DeLorme Publishing Co., 1983.

Hardy, Gerry and Sue Hardy. *Fifty Hikes in Connecticut*. 3rd ed. Woodstock, VT: Backcountry Publications, 1993.

Hicock, Shelton B., ed. *Connecticut Walk Book*. Middletown: Connecticut Forest and Park Association, 1981.

Hill, Evan. *The Connecticut River*. Photography by William F. Stekl. Middletown: Wesleyan University Press, 1972.

Jaques, Florence Page. *Canoe Country*. Minneapolis: University of Minnesota Press, 1938.

Lippincott, Bertram. *Jamestown Sampler*. Ambler, PA: John L. Gaghen & Assoc., 1980.

Mallett, Sandy. *A Year with New England's Birds: A Guide to Twenty-five Field Trips*. Somersworth: New Hampshire Publishing Co., 1978.

Olson, Sigurd F. *Reflections from the North Country*. New York: Alfred A. Knopf, 1976.

Perry, John and Jane Greverus Perry. *The Sierra Club Guide to the Natural Areas of New England*. San Francisco: Sierra Club Books, 1990.

Peterson, Roger Tory. *A Field Guide to the Birds*. 2nd rev. & enl. ed. Boston: Houghton Mifflin, 1960.

Proctor, Noble S. *25 Birding Areas in Connecticut*. Chester, CT: Pequot Press, 1978.

Ritchie, David and Deborah Ritchie. *Connecticut Off the Beaten Path*. Chester, CT: Globe Pequot Press, 1992.

Schroeder, Marion. *Gardening in New England Including New York State: A Resource Guide*. New York: Harper & Row, 1990.

Scull, Theodore. *Water Trips: A Guide to East Coast Cruise Ships, Ferryboats, and Island Excursions*. Camden, ME: International Marine Publishing, 1987.

Sutton, Ann and Myron Sutton. *Eastern Forests*. Audubon Society Nature Guides. New York: Alfred A. Knopf, 1985.

Sutton, Caroline, ed. *The Audubon Society Field Guide to the Natural Places of the Northeast*. Vol. I, Coastal. New York: Pantheon Books, 1984.

Teale, Edwin Way. *A Naturalist Buys an Old Farm*. New York: Dodd, Mead, 1974.

Thoreau, Henry David. *Walden*. New York: Doric Books. Stratford Press, Inc., 1950.

Wass, Stan. *25 Ski Tours in Connecticut*. Somersworth: New Hampshire Publishing Co., 1978.

Weber, Ken. *Canoeing Massachusetts, Rhode Island: and Connecticut*. Woodstock, VT: Backcountry Publications, 1986.

—————. *25 Walks in Rhode Island, A Hiker's Guide to Trails from Buck Hill to Block Island*. Somersworth: New Hampshire Publishing Co., 1978.

Weidensaul, Scott. *Seasonal Guide to the Natural Year: A Month by Month Guide to Natural Events: New England and New York.* Golden, CO: Fulcrum Publishing, 1993.

Wetmore, Alexander. *Song and Garden Birds of North America.* Washington, DC: National Geographic Society, 1964.

Wilson, Alex. *Appalachian Mountain Club Quiet Water Canoe Guide: Massachusetts, Connecticut, Rhode Island: Best Paddling Lakes and Ponds for All Ages.* Boston: Appalachian Mountain Club Books, 1993.

Index

Titles in the Natural Wonders/Green Guide series:

Natural Wonders of Alaska
Natural Wonders of Connecticut & Rhode Island
Natural Wonders of Florida
Green Guide to Hawaii
Natural Wonders of Idaho
Natural Wonders of Massachusetts
Natural Wonders of Michigan
Natural Wonders of New Hampshire
Natural Wonders of New Jersey
Natural Wonders of New York
Natural Wonders of Ohio
Green Guide to Oregon
Natural Wonders of Southern California
Natural Wonders of Texas
Natural Wonders of Vermont
Natural Wonders of Virginia
Green Guide to Washington
Natural Wonders of Wisconsin

All books are $9.95 at bookstores.
Or order directly from the publisher (add $3.00 shipping and
handling for direct orders):

Country Roads Press
P.O. Box 286
Castine, Maine 04421
Toll-free phone number: **800-729-9179**